POEMS TO LEARN
TO READ BY:
Building Literacy With Love

POEMS TO LEARN TO READ BY:
Building Literacy With Love

BETTY S. BARDIGE
and
MARILYN M. SEGAL

ILLUSTRATED BY BERYL SIMON

ZERO TO THREE
PRESS

Washington, DC

Published by

ZERO TO THREE
2000 M St., NW, Suite 200
Washington, DC 20036-3307
(202) 638-1144
Toll-free orders (800) 899-4301
Fax: (202) 638-0851
Web: http://www.zerotothree.org

The mission of the ZERO TO THREE Press is to publish authoritative research, practical resources, and new ideas for those who work with and care about infants, toddlers, and their families. Books are selected for publication by an independent Editorial Board. The views contained in this book are those of the authors and do not necessarily reflect those of ZERO TO THREE: National Center for Infants, Toddlers and Families, Inc.

Cover art: Beryl Simon
Cover design: John Hubbard
Text design and composition: Schawk, Inc.

Library of Congress Cataloging-in-Publication Data

Bardige, Betty Lynn Segal.
    Poems to learn to read by : building literacy with love / Betty S. Bardige and Marilyn M. Segal.
        p. cm.
    Includes index.
    ISBN 0-943657-92-X
    1. Reading (Preschool) 2. Poetry and children. 3. Infants—Books and reading.
4. Education, Preschool—Parent participation. I. Segal, Marilyn M. II. Title.
    LB1140.5.R4B37 2005
    372.4—dc22   2005016026

10 9 8 7 6 5 4 3 2 1
ISBN 0-943657-92-X
Printed in the United States of America

Suggested citation: Bardige, B. S., & Segal, M. M. (2005). *Poems to learn to read by: Building literacy with love*. Washington, DC: ZERO TO THREE Press.

POEMS TO LEARN TO READ BY:
Building Literacy with Love

Teach Me to Read

"Teach me to read!" says Justin,
When I ask what he'd like us to do.
"I need to be cool and important,
So make me a reader, like you."

"Teach me to read," says Justin,
"So I can be grown-up and smart.
If you say that you will, I will try to sit still
And learn all my letters by heart."

"When I can read," says Justin,
"Everything's going to be great.
I will sit at the table and read every label
Before I put food on my plate."

"When my big brother bets he knows something
And he says, 'I can prove it. See—
It's right here in this book!' I will take a good look,
And I'll know if he's just tricking me.

"I will get a big book from the library
And learn something no one else knew.
Then all of the guys will hail Justin the Wise,
'Cause they'll be so amazed that it's true."

"When I want my most favoritest story
And everyone says, 'Not today!'
I'll go to the shelf and get it myself,
And I'll read every page the right way."

"When my neighbors need someone to baby-sit,
My Mom will say, 'Justin's the one!
He keeps kids entertained—reading books, playing games.
You'll be back long before they are done!'"

"I know I can read," says Justin,
"If someone will just show me how.
So don't make me wait. It's almost too late.
I need to start reading right now!"

Justin, at 5 years old, was so eager to learn to read that he begged any willing adult to teach him. He was also quite far along in the process. Growing up in a family that valued reading, Justin naturally wanted to imitate his parents and older brothers. He watched them read newspapers and magazines, reference books and stories, e-mail and greeting cards, product labels, and directions. He knew that reading was something that older children and grown-ups did in their work every day and also for pleasure.

Justin had had many positive experiences with reading. His parents and brothers had been reading to him daily since he was a baby, and he still enjoyed the attention and closeness. He could recognize his favorite books and bring out the ones he wanted to read. He participated in the process by turning pages, asking questions, pointing out pictures and words, sometimes even "reading" a line or speaking in the voice of a character. Justin talked with his parents, brothers, teachers, and friends about things he had learned from books, and they helped him find more books to answer his numerous questions. He was an adept pretender, who acted out stories he had heard and enriched his play with facts and vocabulary that he had learned through reading. As Justin's knowledge grew, so did his ability to ask more complicated questions and understand and appreciate increasingly sophisticated texts.

Through play, reading, and conversation, Justin had learned a lot about words. He knew relatively rare words like *hail, entertained, amazed,* and *spoof,* and could invent a word like *favoritest* when the word he wanted was not in his vocabulary. He understood—intuitively—that words could be made up of parts and that adding or changing a part could change the meaning of a word or how it could be used. Justin also tuned in to the sounds that made up words. He'd had lots of practice with rhyme, alliteration, and other forms of word play, and he could supply a rhyming word or a word that began with a particular sound. Justin understood that words were written with letters and that the letters represented sounds. He could name and write most of the letters of the alphabet.

Justin was well prepared for reading, and it didn't take him long to master it. With a few months of targeted instruction and practice, he was reading independently: enjoying new stories and savoring old favorites, checking labels, and finding intriguing facts. He had learned to love and value reading and could now, on his own, read to learn.

Learning to read begins in early infancy and continues beyond childhood. *Poems to Learn to Read By* celebrates the early phases of this process and provides parents and teachers of young children with tools to support their emerging language and literacy.

Poems to Learn to Read By is really several books in one. It is, first and foremost, a collection of poems for young children and adults to enjoy together. Some of the poems are humorous, some are informative, and some are evocative or instructive. Some tell stories, and others simply play with sounds and words. The poems address the interests, feelings, and questions of young children in words that they can understand and enjoy. Many lend themselves to acting out, singing, chanting, or choral reading.

The poems are also designed to foster emergent literacy. Poetry can be especially powerful in this regard because it highlights the sounds and sound patterns of language. Its short stanzas, rhyme, rhythm, and repetition of sounds make it fun to recite and easy to memorize. The introductions to each chapter highlight parenting and teaching strategies that researchers have found to be effective in building young children's language and literacy skills. Each poem is accompanied by an annotation for parents and teachers. In some cases, the annotations tell the story of the children, experiences, or folk tradition that inspired us to write the poem. They also describe how to use and extend the poem to strengthen children's language, enhance their relationships, and build their literacy skills. Thus, *Poems to Learn to Read By* is also a resource for parents and teachers who are interested in "building literacy with love."

Poems to Learn to Read By is also an *ABC* book. Hidden within its thematically organized chapters are 25 poems that feature particular letters (X shares its poem with W). These poems can be used along with those in Chapter 11 to help children learn the names and sounds of letters, a key step in learning to read. (See page 213, to locate these ABC poems.)

Finally, *Poems to Learn to Read By* is a rich collection of accessible texts for children who are just beginning to read on their own. Although some of the poems deliberately introduce challenging vocabulary, most rely heavily on short, regularly spelled, common words that are easy for beginners to decode. The "easiest" of these are indicated on page 215.

Here Comes Baby!

Literacy begins at birth—perhaps even before! From the moment of birth, babies tune into the world around them. They soon learn to recognize their parents' voices and to focus on things that are interesting to watch, especially the faces of their caregivers. They are primed to connect and communicate. A nursing baby will pause between sucks and lengthen the pause if his mother speaks to him. Her goal may be to keep him eating; his goal seems to be to keep her communicating.

In the first weeks of life, babies recognize and prefer familiar voices and the cadences of familiar languages. Within the first month, they learn to associate a sight with a sound and will turn their heads to see who those approaching footsteps belong to or what made that rattling sound. They soon learn to engage in back-and-forth "conversations," cooing and making faces as they respond to their caregivers' overtures and elicit responses to their own.

As babies interact with the important adults in their lives, they learn to love, to trust, to count on someone responding to their cries, and to predict the effect of their actions. They show interest in things that are "moderately novel," new, but not too strange. As babies gain control over their movements, they begin to explore their environments.

Seeing and hearing, connecting sights and sounds that go together, communicating and conversing, enjoying interaction, curiosity—these are the roots of language and literacy. A tuned-in caregiver who nurtures these roots will be rewarded not only with a baby's delightful accomplishments, but also with her love.

Baby songs and poems play a special role in building these bonds. It is no accident that every culture has a repertoire of songs and poems for babies, including lullabies, nursery rhymes, hand clapping games, peek-a-boo and hide-and-seek rituals, and show-off tricks like "How big is baby? So-o big." Babies love rhythm, rhyme, and melody. They are soothed by gentle crooning and will often kick or bounce to a lively tune.

At the same time, these songs and games provide caregivers with enjoyable ways to play with children, to help them with transitions, and to make daily routines like bathing and dressing opportunities for communication, connection, and learning. Passed down from generation to generation, baby songs are easily learned and long remembered. In families and child-care settings, older children especially enjoy sharing these rituals with babies. Watching or interacting with the older ones, babies get excited and reward their entertainers with a happy smile.

Each relationship a baby develops is special, and she may associate a particular song or game with people. A song from home can help a child-care setting feel more comfortable; a song or game from child care can help parents stay connected to the world their child experiences without them.

Of course, anything you say to a baby can be engaging, as long as you say it in "parentese"—the high-pitched, sing-song way of speaking that parents use when they talk with their babies. A young baby won't understand your words or care whether or not they rhyme. He may get tired before you finish or want you to keep going after your song has ended.

In case you run out of baby songs of your own, we offer this collection for the mutual enjoyment of babies, adults, and older children.

Rock-a-Bye
(to the tune of Rock-a-Bye Baby)

Rock-a-bye baby, in Nana's arms.
You are so cuddly, and so full of charms.
I'll rock you gently, my dear sleepy head,
And put you down softly, in your little bed.

Sweet dreams, my baby.
Have a nice nap.
You'll wake up smiling
And sit on my lap.

Like many lullabies and nursery rhymes, the traditional version of *Rock-a-Bye Baby* is rather violent. Many of these poems and tunes were probably created by older siblings, wet nurses, or indentured servants who may have been a little too eager to get rid of their charges, or at least get them to sleep. You can make up gentler words to these traditional tunes, or just hum over the words you don't like.

Nap Time

Go to sleep, close your eyes,
And I will sing you lullabies.
Pretty baby, you're in luck.
You found your thumb and you can suck.

Wake up time, open your eyes,
And I will give you a surprise.
I will sing your favorite song,
And you'll be happy all day long.

Young babies respond emotionally to internal sensations like hunger and to external sights, sounds, smells, and physical sensations. Indeed, one of their biggest challenges is regulating their emotional state. They can't learn when they are too keyed up—crying, overly excited, agitated and flailing, fearful or stressed. They also can't learn when they are tuned out—asleep, depressed, lethargic, droopy, or shut down. Most of their learning occurs during a quiet, alert state when they can focus their attention outside of themselves and mobilize their energy for action.

Babies count on adults to help them keep their emotions within bounds—to feed them when they are hungry and comfort them when they are upset, but also to intrigue and engage them when they are ready to play. It's a subtle dance. As baby and adult get to know each other, the baby gives moment-to-moment cues about what she needs. She may look at the adult intently, imitate facial expressions, smile or coo or laugh in response to what the adult does. She may turn away briefly to take a break, then come back for more. When she's had too much, she may curl her toes, arch her back, fuss, cry, or show other signs of stress, or she may simply shut down and go to sleep.

Sucking a thumb or pacifier is one way that babies can comfort themselves when they experience distress, need to discharge excess energy, or transition between sleep and wakefulness. When they need help, they may respond to a slow, quiet, soothing voice and gentle rocking or patting, or to a livelier beat and more vigorous rocking or bouncing.

Make up your own tune for this lullaby. You may want to use the first verse as you put the baby to sleep, and the second verse as you help her maintain equilibrium as she wakes up.

Here Comes Baby! • **5**

Baby Babbles

Ba-ba
Ba-ba boo
You love me and I love you.

Ma-ma
Ma-ma, Mummy
You are such a little honey.

Da-da
Da-da, Dad
You make Daddy very glad.

Make sure that the baby watches your face as you say or sing this poem. Pause for a few seconds after each line to see if the baby will chime in.

Respond to babies' attempts at babbling by imitating their sounds and facial expressions, then pausing to see if they will repeat their babbles. When babies get good at this game, vary the sounds and see if they will imitate you.

Baby Songs

Babies listen when you're singing.
They listen when a bell is ringing.
They clap their hands and kick their feet
In perfect rhythm to the beat.

As you sing this song, help the baby clap his hands and feet.

Tickle, Tickle

Tickle tummy, tickle ear.
You are such a little dear.
Tickle tummy, tickle toes.
Now I'll tickle your little nose.

Tickle each part of the baby as you touch him.

Changing Table Fun

Spread out Baby's arms.
Now touch Baby's nose.
Stretch out Baby's legs.
Now clap Baby's toes.

Kiss my baby's tummy.
Fix my baby's hair.
Now snap up the pretty clothes
That Baby likes to wear.

Diaper changing and dressing provide great opportunities to converse with babies and to share poems, songs, and ritual exercises. A good time to share this poem is when a baby is almost all dressed. You can act out each line, then end with a kiss or hug as you lift the baby off of the changing table.

You may also want to make up your own poems—the baby won't notice if they don't rhyme—to accompany your movements as you change and dress the baby. Be sure to engage the baby's attention as you talk to him and to pause whenever he has something to say and whenever he looks away or signals that he needs a break.

Getting to Know You

Here are your hands.
Here are your toes.
Here is your mouth,
And here is your nose.

Here are your cheeks.
Here is your chin.
These are your eyes.
Now show me a grin.

I love you
With no if or maybe.
Because you are
My sweet little baby.

Touch baby's hands, toes, and so forth as you chant or sing. You may want to repeat the first two verses, substituting "my" for "your" and helping the baby touch or point to parts of your face and body.

Cooing

I'll tell your daddy
That it is true.
You're really talking
When you coo-oo.

So coo, coo my baby
All the day long,
And I will sing you
A coo-cooing song.

When you are bigger,
Then you will know
How to sing high and
How to sing low.

So sing, sing my baby
All the day long.
As you are singing
I'll sing along.

Let baby watch your lips as you say or sing this poem. Watch her face, too, and pause whenever she has something to say. Remember, engaging her in back-and-forth conversation is much more important than finishing the poem.

You might also share the poem with others who care for and interact with the baby, so as to help them appreciate the baby's emerging language and the importance of engaging her in very frequent "conversations."

Playing Together

Up, up my baby goes.
Here are your fingers and here are your toes.
Here is your tummy and here is your knee.
Now how about a smile for me?

Pull the baby gently up to a sitting position. Bring her hands together so that she touches her fingers, then touch her hands to her toes, tummy, and knees as you name each part. Bring her hands to your face as you say the last line with a big smile.

When You're Happy

When you smile
I am happy.
Now it's time for
Clappedy, clappy.

I put you down.
I pull you up.
I let you drink
From your sippy cup.

Help baby clap to your singing.

See-saw

See-saw, Marjorie Daw,
Soon you will have a new master.
Toss your teddy out of the way
And then you can go so much faster.

Babies who have learned to sit up will enjoy this variation on the traditional rhyme. Hold baby's hands as you take turns leaning back and forth. Speed up on the last line. You can help babies who are learning to sit by providing just as much help pulling them up as they need.

Bumpedy Bump

Bumpedy bump
On your rump.
Let's keep bumping all day long
While I sing you this bumping song.

Chant this as you bounce the baby on your knees.

Trot, Trot

Trot, trot to Boston.
Trot, trot to Lynn.
Watch out Baby
Or you might fall . . . **in.**

Trot, trot to Boston.
Trot, trot so slow.
Now let's gallop very fast.
See my Baby go!

Bounce baby on your knees as you recite this traditional poem. We've added a second verse for variety. You can use the verses separately or together.

In the first verse, open your legs a bit on "in" so that the baby gets a surprise (and very small) "fall." After several repetitions of the first verse, the baby will learn to anticipate the "in."

With the second verse, begin bouncing at a moderate pace, slow down almost to a stop as you say the second line, then bounce as fast as you can for the last two lines.

Look at Baby

Up, up, up goes Baby—
Going up so high.
Look, look, look at Baby.
See my baby fly.

Turn, turn, turn goes Baby.
Spin my baby round.
Down, down, down goes Baby—
Right down to the ground.

Look into the baby's eyes as you say this poem. When you say "up," lift the baby up in your arms. When you say "fly," hold the baby up in the air, swinging her gently. When you say "turn" and "spin around," turn around as you hold baby in your arms. Put the baby down when you say "down." Repeat the poem if the baby bounces or picks up her arms to show that she wants more.

Yeah, Hooray for Baby

Yeah, hooray for Baby—
Look what she can do.
She can find her daddy's nose.
She can touch her shoe.

Yeah, hooray for Baby—
She can read her book.
She can stand up by herself.
She can help me cook.

Yeah, hooray for Baby—
Banging on her pan.
Can she make a big loud noise?
Yes, my baby can!

Encourage older children to help you make up additional verses to celebrate the baby's accomplishments.

CHAPTER
2

Feelings and Choices

The toddler and preschool years are critical to literacy. This is the time when children learn to speak, and then learn to "use their words" to make choices, express feelings, and solve problems. Children who hear many more "yeses" than "nos" during this time are ahead of the game. Research shows that they not only develop the confidence and curiosity to explore new territory and take on new challenges, but they also develop significantly larger vocabularies than do children who are scolded more often and praised or encouraged less frequently. Similarly, when parents and caregivers offer children choices, rather than simply telling them what to do, the children hear and practice more and richer language. As a consequence, they develop larger vocabularies and greater capacity to "use their words."

Giving children choices also supports their emotional development. Toddlers are developing an awareness of themselves as separate people with their own wishes and preferences and the ability to make other people pay attention. *No, more,* and *want* are likely to be among their early words. When a 2-year-old says "no," he is demonstrating the fact that he is his own person and has a right to make choices. At times, he may say "no" in order to assert himself even when he really means "yes." It is not unusual for a 2-year-old to say "no" when asked if he wants a cookie and then get angry when his parent doesn't give it to him. Another favorite toddler expression is "me do it myself." Although, a child who insists on putting on his own sweater with no help can be annoying to a caregiver who is trying to take the class outside, this desire to be independent is an important toddler development.

The preschool years bring dramatic advances in emotional development. These changes reflect the child's increased ability to control his own emotions and his increased awareness of other people's feelings. Preschoolers learn to use language to express their feelings, negotiate with others, and talk themselves through challenges. At the same time, a new capacity to pretend and imagine brings new fears. The line between fantasy and reality is likely to be quite blurred.

Poems and stories can affirm children's feelings and model creative solutions to common issues and problems. Seeing a character who is exaggeratedly stubborn, willful, or awkward puts their own behavior in perspective. Similarly, because young children's fears grow out of their magical, prelogical thinking, they are quite susceptible to magical resolutions. Seeing a storybook monster vanquished with an invisible sword or tamed with a magic word, a child learns how she can control the truly frightening monsters of her own imagination.

When parents and teachers take a playful approach—using fantasy and humor to redirect children's activities or smooth over rough spots—children learn that there is more than one way to solve a problem. At the same time, they gain practice in expressive language and storytelling.

For playful parents, caring teachers, and young children with strong feelings, we offer this collection of child-affirming poems and positive discipline ideas. Several of these poems, as the annotations suggest, can also be used to enhance other aspects of literacy, such as writing, story interpretation, and alphabet knowledge.

All About Me

Would you like to know about me?
I have two eyes so I can see.
And when I look up in the sky
I see the blackbirds passing by.

I have two ears so I can hear
The happy sounds when people cheer,
The sad sound of a baby's cry
And the music of a lullaby.

I have a nose so I can smell.
When something stinks, my nose can tell.
I like the smells of fresh-baked bread
And roses in their flower bed.

I have a tongue so I can taste
Chocolate pudding and red bean paste,
Sour lemons and salty fish,
And all the flavors in each dish.

I have ten fingers so I can feel
The smoothness of an apple peel,
The softness of a baby's hair,
And my favorite fluffy teddy bear.

This poem celebrates a child's emerging sense of herself and her delight in exploring the world with all of her senses. As you share it with children, ask them to show you their two eyes, two ears, nose, tongue, and ten fingers. Talk together about the things they like to see, hear, smell, taste, and feel as well as some of the things they don't like.

I Won't Eat My Lunch

I won't eat my lunch
And you can't make me do it.
I will spit out the hot dog
Because I can't chew it.

I hate all the spinach.
The liver is worst.
If you make me eat it,
My tummy will burst.

I won't even look
At that caramel custard.
And I'll only eat French fries
With ketchup and mustard.

If you give me some yogurt
With sprinkles on top,
I will eat just four bites
And then I will stop.

Many parents and teachers of toddlers and preschoolers will recognize the narrator of this poem. No matter what is offered for a meal, the child has some complaint. The carrots are no good because they touched the peas, the yogurt can only be eaten with rainbow sprinkles, or the sandwich can't have even a trace of crust or has to be cut into triangles instead of squares. One day's favorite food may be rejected the next.

The real issue, of course, is control. The child is learning to make choices and to use his words to make his preferences known. Offering choices helps you build the child's self-esteem and language skills: "What would you like to drink with your sandwich?" "Should I cut the cheese into squares or triangles?" "How many pieces of apple would you like?" and "Should I make the rice sticky or fluffy?"

continued

After sharing the poem with children, you might ask them to talk about the foods they like and the foods they don't like. Is their anything alike about those they love or those they hate? Do some foods come up on everyone's lists?

A fun activity to do with a group of preschoolers is to make a bar graph of favorite foods. Start by helping children find pictures of favorite foods in grocery store ads or use stickers with pictures of different foods. On a large piece of paper, create a graph with a column for each food. Place a picture of the food at the bottom of the column and write its name underneath. Let children take turns coloring in a square on the graph (or pasting a sticker in the square) for each food that they like. Show them how to fill in the columns from the bottom up, using a different color (or sticker) for each food. When they are finished, the class will be able to see which foods are the most and least popular. Some children will enjoy counting how many "votes" the different foods received.

My Don't-Like List

I don't like strawberries and I don't like stew.
I don't like oysters when they're turning blue.
I don't like broccoli and I won't eat steak
And green beans give me a tummy ache.

I hate asparagus and I can't stand cheese.
I won't eat carrots if they're mixed with peas.
I won't eat a sandwich if it has a crust
And I won't nibble celery—unless I must.

I spit out cabbage and I choke on soup.
I won't taste oatmeal 'cause it looks like goup.
And if there's some yucky food I missed,
Just add it to my don't-like list.

One way to help picky eaters is to help them make a don't-like list. If a food is on the list, they don't have to eat it. If a food is not on the list, they have to taste it before deciding whether they like it or don't like it. After creating a don't-like list, picky eaters can be encouraged to make lists of foods that they do like. Some will enjoy watching the list grow as they discover more and more foods that they like.

Of course, making like lists and don't like lists is also a great literacy activity, and one that all children can enjoy. Cut pictures of foods from magazines, catalogs, and grocery store ads, and let children sort them into "like" and "don't like" piles. You can write the words for them or write them out and let them copy them onto their lists. Children might also enjoy making books of favorite foods or putting together a menu of favorites (or of choices they think of as silly or disgusting) for a pretend restaurant.

Clothes

I won't wear that dress to school.
I know I'm as stubborn as a mule.
I won't wear a raincoat unless it is sunny,
And I won't stop spending too much money.

I won't wear those glasses. They make me look queer.
And I won't try them on until next year.
I won't wear pajamas, and I won't wear shoes,
And I won't wear anything I did not choose.

Giving children the opportunity to choose their own clothes (within reason) can help avoid family hassles. It's also a great way to introduce color, shape, size, fabric, and texture words into their conversation. Children may also enjoy choosing clothes for a class doll or puppet or selecting dress-up costumes. Encourage them to use specific language to describe their choices.

After sharing this poem, talk with children about what kinds of clothes they like to wear on different occasions, to different places, and in different kinds of weather. Who helps them decide what to wear?

Another approach would be to use a puppet or doll as the narrator of the poem. Read the poem in the puppet's voice, then have the children help the puppet find appropriate things to wear. As you play the part of the puppet, you'll have an opportunity to use specific language as you accept and reject the children's suggestions. "I don't like that wool sweater. It's scratchy and it makes me hot and itchy. Oh, thank you. I love these purple corduroy pants. They're all loose and baggy—just the way I like them!"

Getting Dressed

Do you suppose that a sock on your nose
Would be good for wearing today?
And by any chance would your blue underpants
Look nice on your eyes while you play?

Would a bathing suit look kind of cute
Worn upside down on your knee?
Would your pajama top make traffic stop
If you waved it about with glee?

Would a shoe on your ear help you to hear
Everything everyone said?
Would a raincoat be right for wearing tonight
When you jump right into your bed?

Can you show me how you dress yourself now
With your socks and your shoes on your toes?
And your clothes for the day put on just the right way
With each piece in the place that it goes?

This poem was written for a 3-year-old who hated to get dressed but loved
word play and silliness. Whenever he refused to put on his clothes or let his
mother do it, she would recite a few lines, and soon he'd chime in with an
absurd idea of his own. With the tension broken, getting dressed changed
from a battle to a game.

Bed Time

"It's time for bed," said Nana.
"Come on, now. Don't be slow.
Here's your nice new nightgown."
But Nellie said,
"No. No."

"Here's your teddy bear," said Nana.
Now up to bed you go."
Please put on your nightgown."
But Nellie said,
"No. No."

"No nightgown for you," said Nana.
"You can sleep in clothes, I guess.
Do you need a good night story?"
Then Nellie said,
"Yes. Yes."

Most young children resist going to bed at times, and Nellie is no exception. Nellie's Nana finds that giving Nellie some choices is more effective than simply telling her what to do.

Preschoolers who enjoy the poem might like to make their own bedtime books—filled with pictures and words of things that they "need" before they can go to sleep. You might help children get started by writing "Bedtime, by _____" on the cover and then writing "Before I go to sleep, I need" on the first page. Children can then add their own drawings, photographs, or pictures cut from magazines and catalogs to the other pages. You might write "Good night" on the last page or on the back of the book.

You can also use this poem to help children learn to recognize the letter N and associate it with its sound. In the poem, whose names start with N? Who else do children know whose names start with N? What other N words can they find in the poem?

My Bad Awful Day

I've had a terrible awful day.
Nothing seemed to go my way.
I didn't have anything to do.
That's why I had to trouble you.

You sat down and drank your tea
And did not give one drop to me.
You did not buy me a candy cane,
And you would not let me walk in the rain.

You didn't buy me a single thing—
Not even one small friendship ring.
It was a terrible, awful day,
And now I am going to run away.

I am packing my bag and putting in Teddy,
And after that I will be all ready.
But there's one more thing that I can't miss.
I really need my goodnight kiss.

From a child's point of view, little things can ruin or make a day, but what counts in the end is the attention, affection, and recognition that they receive from the important adults in their lives.

Talking about the good—and bad—things that happened is a nice way to end a day, an activity, or a project. As they talk about their memories of recent events, children are strengthening memory and storytelling skills. They are using what literacy researchers call "decontextualized language;" that is, language that goes beyond the here and now. Children who get plenty of practice talking about their own past experiences and future plans are likely to enjoy the decontextualized language of storybooks and to develop robust vocabularies and strong emergent literacy skills.

How to Have a Temper Tantrum

How to have a tantrum
Is something every child should know.
If you don't know, I can teach you.
I'm a temper tantrum pro.

With my kind of tantrum, there's nothing to fear.
I can do it without even shedding a tear.
Are you ready to try a tantrum now?
Then listen up! I will tell you how.

First wave your arms up in the air
With all the power you can spare.
The next thing to do is to stamp your feet.
Stamp so hard you break up the street.

Then after that you can gurgle and rumble,
Shout "grump, grr-rump," and then start to grumble.
When you can't grumble for one minute more,
Give one last grr-rump and fall on the floor.

Now let out a really ear-splitting scream
Just as loud as a whole football team.
Scream so loud that you're certain to scare
All of the people everywhere.

Then be real quiet for a second or two
To make sure that somebody's watching you.
You'll know that your tantrum was perfectly done
When you get the attention of everyone.

---

continued

Toddlers are known for temper tantrums, but most children learn to control these outbursts by the time they are 3 or 4. One way to help is with humor. The author of this poem has trained a slew of children, grandchildren, and students in her temper tantrum technique. Make sure that you choose a time to teach "temper tantrumming" when everyone is having a good day. Then, when a child is about to tantrum, remind her of the "right" way to do it. If you have given children a chance to practice acting out this poem—and to realize how silly a tantrum can look—most real tantrums will change into laughter.

There's a Monster Under My Bed

There is a monster under my bed.
I saw his tail and part of his head.
But when Dad came to kiss me goodnight,
He hurried and scurried out of sight.

Of course you know I'm not afraid
Of all the noise that monster made.
And I really think I'd be all right,
If Dad did not turn off the light.

Tomorrow when I go to bed,
I'll wear pajamas that are bright red.
When the monster sees my pajamas I'll shout,
"Red means danger, so you better get out!"

The rich imaginations that make preschoolers such good pretenders and avid storytellers during the day can haunt them at night. Poems like these, and classic story books like *Where the Wild Things Are,* can help children to cope with their nighttime fears. You might talk together about the children in the poems. What do they see and hear? What frightens them? Is it real or pretend? How do they make the scary monster or nightmare go away? Children might like to talk about their own night time fears. Is there anything that scares them (or that they used to be scared of when they were little)? What do they do to scare that scary thing away?

Some children might like to make their own nighttime books. You can help by providing black construction paper to use as a background for the pages. Children can draw and write directly on the black paper or paste on drawings, words, and magazine cutouts. You might give them prompts to get them started:

- Sometimes at night _____.
- It's scary when _____.
- I'm NOT scared because _____.

Encourage children to dictate words to you or help those with an interest to write (or scribble) themselves and then read back their stories to them.

Dreaming

What was it that I dreamed last night
That gave me such a terrible fright?
I tried to figure out what to do
If someone had run away with you.

I searched in my bedroom, and I searched in the hall,
And then I made a telephone call.
I called the police so I could find out
If my mother had gone. Then I started to shout.

The policeman told me to quiet down.
It wasn't right to wake up the town.
But I had to shout cause my mother was lost,
And I had to find her at any cost.

I ran back to my house and she was there,
Sitting in her rocking chair.
"You must have had a nightmare," she said.
Then she gave me a kiss and tucked me in bed.

I'm Angry Today

I'm angry today.
Latisha took my truck away.
And then she said I couldn't play.
I'm angry today.

I'm angry today.
I tried to make a horse of clay.
Its head fell off—it wouldn't stay—
I'm angry today.

I'm angry today.
I pound and pound and pound the clay
To make a mask that seems to say
"I'm angry today."

I'm angry today.
I put on my mean mask and say,
"Rrr, rrr, rrr—you get away!
I'm angry today!"

I'm angry today.
Latisha comes and joins my play.
We roar so loud we scare our prey.
We're lions today.

The child in the poem finds constructive and playful ways to express her anger and frustration. Can children identify these strategies? A group of children who enjoy this poem might like to discuss what they do when they get angry with a friend or with themselves. They might also like to talk about what makes them angry or what else the child in the poem could have done to solve his problem.

The poem could also be used to introduce a mask-making activity. Children might make different animal masks from clay or papier-mâché or from paper plates or paper bags. They could also make masks that show different emotions.

Temper Tantrums

I have a terrible temper.
I do get very mad.
Would you like to hear about
The worst tantrum I had?

Last night when I was playing with
My favorite Winnie the Pooh,
His ear fell off, so I stuck it back
With a little Crazy Glue.

I knew my Pooh was dirty,
And I tried to make him clean.
I washed his toes and scrubbed his nose
I tried not to be mean.

And just to get him whiter
I covered him with salt.
The salt fell on the kitchen floor,
But it was not my fault.

And then I had a new idea.
I let him play with clay.
When Mother saw the mess I'd made,
She took my bear away.

Of course I had a tantrum.
There was nothing else to do.
How could Mother take away
My favorite Winnie the Pooh?

Then Dad said, "Stop your howling.
Your Pooh will be just fine
After he swims in the washing machine
And hangs out on the line."

This poem gains its humor by playing on the difference between a child's logic and feelings and those of his parents. It also provides an opportunity to talk with children: both about what happens in the poem and about their own feelings and experiences.

As you read this poem with children, talk with them about what is happening in each verse and how the child is feeling. Does he take good care of his Pooh? Did he mean to get salt on the floor and clay all over Pooh? What did he think his mother was going to do when she took Pooh away? How did he feel then? What did his mother really do? How do you think the boy felt when his father explained that Pooh would be fine?

You can also help children connect the poem to their own experiences. Who has a favorite doll or stuffed animal? Can they tell about it? Did their "friend" ever get dirty or lost? What happened? How did they feel?

Chicken Pox

I guess I have the chicken pox.
My back is all itchy and my head's full of rocks.
There are lumps on my tummy and bumps on my head,
And Mother told me to stay in my bed.

My father told me that I should stop scratching.
He said chicken pox is not worth catching.
He put on my pajamas and some very high socks
And told me not to worry about chicken pox.

Dad told me my pox would soon go away,
But I had to stay in bed all day.
He told me again that I should not scratch,
Or the chicken's eggs were likely to hatch.

The very next day I got out of bed,
And the spots were no longer itching my head.
I got out of bed and I started to play,
And the poxes and blotches all went away.

Making cards for sick classmates is a great literacy activity.

Boasting

I'm the best girl in town.
I always smile and never frown.
I am always happy when I win
Any contest that I'm in.

I'm good at everything I do.
Anyone you ask will say it's true.
I love to sing. I love to dance
Whenever I can get a chance.

I'm so much smarter than the boys.
I'm good at making clever toys.
I'm as grand as I can be—
So everyone, please clap for me.

The girl in this poem may be a bit too boastful, but every child has something to be proud of. Young children who sense that the important people in their life are proud of them rarely become boastful. Instead, they develop a healthy sense of self-esteem and a willingness to try new things and to keep trying until they succeed. When praise is genuine, children will work hard to earn it.

All By Myself

I took my teddy off the shelf.
I took him down all by myself,
Because I'm getting very tall—
Just yesterday I was too small.

I ate my Jell-O with a spoon,
And then I played all afternoon.
And when I finished with my playing,
I picked up my toys without Mom saying.

When you finish reading this poem to children, you might want to encourage them to join you in clapping for the child it describes. You can then talk together about the things they can do "all by themselves."

Young children especially enjoy books about themselves, and an easy way to create one is to take pictures of the child doing things she enjoys or has just mastered. Then you can read the book together, letting her tell the story of her accomplishments.

CHAPTER 3

Families and Friends

Toddlers spend a lot of time talking with adults. Parents, trusted caregivers, and older siblings can understand their grunts, babbles, and gestures as well as their early attempts to use words. Because these adults can guess what the toddler means, they can fill in the missing pieces of the conversation. Adults can also be patient and are willing to follow a child's lead. Watching a toddler at play, an adult can offer a comment and wait for the child to respond. When the toddler says a word or two (or something that sounds like a word), an adult can restate what the child seemed to be saying, add a comment or question, and encourage the child to say more. These early conversations are the foundation of language and literacy. They also help toddlers learn how to make friends.

Once children master language, they will talk to everyone—including their peers, dolls, and imaginary friends. These conversations give them the opportunity to practice and extend their language skills as they make connections, share information and ideas, entice playmates to join them, negotiate roles, play out imaginary scenarios, plan joint activities and projects, and patch up inevitable rifts. One of the best ways to support young children's early literacy is to include them in family conversations and to encourage their conversations with peers.

As they interact with family and friends, young children learn to be helpful, share and take turns, cooperate, and resolve conflicts. Each new friend they play with gives them an opportunity to share new experiences, learn new games, share ideas, pretend, imagine, and create. As they play with a friend, children learn to cooperate, to appreciate differences, and to find new ways to make discoveries and expand their horizons. As they play together, children learn the importance of sharing. They learn to explore things from a different perspective and to build on each other's ideas. They learn trust, caring, and respect, and they come to recognize and value interdependence.

Poems and stories about families and friends can help children appreciate other people's feelings and learn words to say when conflicts arise. Because families and friends are so important, we offer this collection of poems that celebrate relationships.

My Family

I have the best family there ever could be
'Cause everyone likes to play with me.
My sister likes to rub my head.
She lets me jump up on her bed.

My father lets me help him cook.
My brother reads me my favorite book.
My grandpa takes me on long walks
So he and I can have long talks.

My uncle throws me in the air.
My grandma takes me everywhere!
My baby likes to hold my hand.
My mother tells me I am grand.

My cousins let me win our races
And laugh when I make funny faces.
They all tell stories they swear are true
About the silly things I used to do.

So whether your family is big or small,
Six brothers and sisters—or none at all.
I hope you think it is really great
And have lots of things to celebrate!

Every family has lots of things to celebrate. A child's first and most cherished book is often a family album with pictures of the important people in her life. These may include relatives and close family friends, whether they live with her or even live nearby. For many young children, pets are also an important part of the family. As you read a family album together, help a toddler point to particular people and say their names. Talk with a 2-year-old about what is happening in the pictures and help her remember recent events. Encourage preschoolers to tell you stories that are prompted by their family albums and to make their own family pictures and scrapbooks.

Fighting

My little sister loves to fight.
She threw a pillow at me last night.
She tossed her toys all over the floor,
Then she left the room and slammed the door.

I don't like it when my sister sings
Or messes up my favorite things.
Or when she tries on all my clothes
Or steps down hard on my poor toes.

I hate it when she calls me names
Or takes the pieces from my games.
I ask her not to make a mess,
But that is hard for her, I guess.

My sister isn't really bad,
Even though she makes me mad.
I know I would not want any other
To be my sister's favorite brother.

Sibling relationships are often filled with both love and rivalry. This poem gives children a chance to talk about both as they share the things that they like to do with their siblings and friends as well as the things that bug them.

In a family child-care home or a multiage center classroom, the children can become like a family, where older children help out and teach younger ones but also need time and space to themselves. Encouraging both mixed-age activities and separate reading and writing work for older children can have many benefits for literacy. Older children can model an interest in reading and writing; they can also improve their own skills as they share books with younger ones. Younger children—even babies—can join older ones in songs and movement games as well as pretend play. Their delight at being included encourages older children to play nurturing roles. At the same time, watching older children engage in more grownup reading and writing activities gives younger ones something to look forward to.

Friendship

I went to school the other day.
I told my mom I would not stay.
But Amanda said, "Let's have some fun.
C'mon, I'll show you how it's done."

We went outside to play in the sand.
I tripped on a tree root and she held my hand.
She told me that she loved to bake
And made me a sandy birthday cake.

Then we both went down the slide.
She always stayed close by my side.
I didn't want the day to end.
School is fine when you have a friend.

Young children—even toddlers—can be very good friends. They often seem to know instinctively what another child needs and how to provide comfort or reassurance. You might like to share this poem with a few children who are close friends. Do they remember how they first got to be friends? What are their favorite things to do together?

Taking Turns

When you're doing something you really like,
Like pumping a swing or riding a bike,
The hardest thing you have to learn
Is to stop and give a friend a turn.
But when her turn is over, then
It can be your turn again.
When you're playing together, you have to be fair.
Turns are something you have to share.

Taking turns is a challenge for very young children. They are not usually very good at waiting, and somehow their turn always seems to go by too fast while other people's turns seem to take forever. Some parents and teachers use a timer to help children wait. Setting the timer and watching it turn gives the waiting child something to do and provides an opportunity to learn concepts like "second," "minute," and "almost." Children are often more willing to wait when they have some control over the process, and are more willing to give up a turn when signaled by a bell than when ordered by an impatient playmate.

Turn taking is the essence of conversation. Babies learn it early, as they babble and coo at a parent or caregiver who babbles and coos back at them. Carrying on a real conversation is much harder, of course, and young children often follow their own rules. They may ignore a comment directed at them, especially if it is a request that they would rather not fulfill. They may also change the subject abruptly to one that is more to their liking, or they may jabber away without giving anyone else a turn to talk.

Group conversations can be especially challenging. Some children have a lot to say and want to monopolize the discussion. Others patiently wait their turns, but may forget what they wanted to say before they can get a chance to say it. Still others lose interest or change the subject. Small groups of three to five people make conversations much easier, especially when children are engaged in a joint project or game.

A Friend-ly Fight

"You had a long ride and it's my turn next.
If you won't listen, I will be quite vexed.
Get off of that bike! Give it to me now!
If you don't get off, I will show you how."

"No," said my friend, "You can't have your way.
Remember how nasty you were yesterday?
You were even nastier the day before,
So I'm not going to be your friend anymore!"

My dad came out when he heard our spat.
He said, "You guys shouldn't yell like that."
He told us we had to make amends
So that we could continue to be good friends.

"I'm sorry," I said, "that I got mad
At the most fun friend I've ever had."
My friend smiled and said, "That's OK.
I'm sorry, too. Now let's go play."

Conflict is common in most young children's friendships, just as it is between siblings. Most of the time, children can resolve these conflicts without adult help. Doing so gives them a chance to use their words and develop their negotiation skills. At times, though, an adult needs to intervene to help children calm down and find the words that will enable them to solve the problem and repair the relationship.

Most children will be able to tell you a story about a disagreement with a friend. Talk with them about what it means to "make amends." What did the children in the poem do? What else could they have done?

Sandbox Fun

Our vase was full of water.
Our pail was full of sand.
We dumped them in the sandbox
To make a vast new land.

First we built a village,
And then we made a town.
We scooped out a volcano,
But it was upside down.

We shoveled out a valley
Between two mountains tall.
We poured a little river.
Now we have a waterfall!

Our hands are very dirty.
Our sleeves are very wet.
But we are very happy
With our best creation yet!

This poem was inspired by a true story. The two friends got so busy shoveling a hole in their "volcano" that they dug out their mountain and hit the bottom of the sandbox. Rather than starting over, they simply declared—with great delight—that they had built an upside down volcano!

A sandbox is an especially good setting for conversation. Children can play on their own or together and talk about what they are making. Even children who don't set out to build something together will often find a way to connect their constructions.

After sharing the poem with children, talk with them about what they like to make in the sandbox. What can they add to the sandbox to make sand play more fun?

Children who are learning their letters may enjoy searching for Vs in this poem. Which words have a V at the beginning? Which ones have a V in the middle or near the end? Does anyone have a V in their name?

Sharing

This is my candy and I want it all.
I'm sure it will make me grow up to be tall.
I have to get strong. I need to get big
In case there's a tunnel that I want to dig.

I won't give you any, not even a bite.
I'm saving the rest to eat late at night.
I like eating candy. I want to get fat.
And I know that you don't have an answer to that!

But my sister said I was not being fair.
If I have some candy, I really should share.
She said, "If you give me just one piece to chew,
Next time I get some, I will give one to you."

This poem captures a conversation between siblings who are having trouble sharing. With younger children, you may have to explain that candy doesn't make you "grow up to be tall" or help you get big and strong. Older children will understand that the narrator is just making excuses for not sharing.

After reading this poem with children, you might want to talk with them about what they are—and are not—willing to share. What will they do if the child they shared something with doesn't give it back? When was the last time one of their friends shared something important, like a secret, with them?

My Favorite Toy

I have a yellow yo-yo,
And I can make it go
Down and up and round the world.
Yes, either fast or slow.

Would you like to use my yo-yo?
You can try to make it sleep.
The yo-yo is yours to use today,
But it is mine to keep.

Sharing a favorite toy can be difficult for young children. Words can help: "You can use it, but you have to give it back" or "I'm just going to borrow it for a little while." After a while, they learn that sharing goes both ways, and that most toys are a lot more fun when you share them with friends. After reading this poem with children, you might talk with them about their favorite toys and books. Which ones do they like to keep for themselves? Which ones are more fun to use with a friend or sibling?

As you share this poem with children, you might also take the opportunity to share some stories from your childhood. What were your favorite toys? Did you have a yo-yo? Could you do any tricks?

For children who are learning letters, this poem can be used to talk about the letter Y. The letter Y is fairly easy to recognize and draw, but in other ways it is quite tricky. Even its name is misleading—it starts with a /w/ sound. In most words with Ys in them, the Y is silent (as in *today*) or is pronounced as a vowel (as in *my*). However, Y also has a consonant sound at the beginning of words or syllables (as in *yellow, yo-yo,* and *yours*), although this same sound is heard in words with Us but no Ys, such as *use* and *cucumber.* Children who speak Spanish will also hear the /y/ sound in words that begin with a double L.

It takes a while for readers to master these nuances. For beginners, it's enough to notice that Ys are found in all kinds of words, like *yellow, Happy Birthday,* and, perhaps, in the names of some of their friends.

Imaginary Friend

I have a friend you cannot see.
No one plays with him but me.
My friend stays close wherever we go,
And my friend never tells me no.

My friend's name is Mickledy Mike.
He likes to play the things I like.
I share my secrets. He does, too,
Because that is what all good friends do.

I never have a thing to fear,
'Cause Mickledy Mike is always here.
He never runs away from me.
He's as faithful as a friend could be.

It is quite common for young children to have imaginary friends. When parents and caregivers take these friendships seriously, the child is encouraged to invent more and more elaborate stories about the friend's exploits. Some children insist that their friends are not imaginary at all—they are just invisible. Either way, as the child weaves her tales and as adults encourage her by asking questions or by conversing with the "friend" ("Oh. You'd like pizza for breakfast? Is that what you said? I think we might have some."), she is developing the rich, playful language and enjoyment of fantasy that will prepare her to be a successful and avid reader.

Hairy Harry

Hairy Harry is my friend.
He's happy as can be.
Just when I want to play with him,
He wants to play with me.

Hairy Harry loves to fly.
He likes to up and go.
So when I want to throw him high,
He never says, "No, no."

If Harry hops onto the floor
Or drops down in the dirt,
You will not hear him cry or roar.
He never does get hurt.

In case you can't guess, Hairy Harry is a stuffed cat. He belongs to a little boy who carries him everywhere and won't go to sleep—or anywhere new and a little scary—without him. The boy thinks of Harry as a friend, and often talks to him and includes him in his pretend play. However, his favorite thing to do with Harry is to throw him around—as high or far as he can.

Because Harry is such a constant companion, the child's parents often use him to help their son with transitions. If the boy is reluctant to go to a new place, his father reassures Harry and tells him how much fun it's going to be. When the boy gets too wild and Harry's "flying lessons" get out of hand, Harry has to sit on a high shelf "until you feel calmer and are ready to play nicely." When the child resists going to bed, his mother enlists his help in putting Harry to sleep.

Children who like this poem may enjoy telling stories about their own stuffed animals or dolls. They might even make them presents of home-made picture books (featuring the animal or doll and the things he or she likes to do), which they can "read" to them. As children pretend to read, they are practicing the book-handling skills and storybook language that they will use when they read "for real."

In a classroom setting, a puppet or doll that is treated as a member of the class can play the same role that Hairy Harry does at home. When the room is a mess and the children don't want to clean up, when a child has hurt another child's feelings, or when some children seem to be a little bit worried about an upcoming field trip, a public conversation with the class puppet can engage children in solving the problem, help them express concerns without embarrassment, or provide needed reassurance.

Kate's Best Friends

I have a friend named Katie
Who is very much like me.
We dress our dolls in princess clothes
And serve them oolong tea.

We make up funny stories
And act out all the parts.
We draw each other pictures
With rainbows, stars, and hearts.

We like to play with board games—
The kind that have a spinner.
We face challenges along the path
And don't care who's the winner.

I have a friend named Kaitlin
Who loves to climb and run.
My mom thinks Kaitlin is kind of rough
But I think she is fun.

Kaitlin makes up stories
Full of danger and suspense.
She always wants to build tree forts
Or climb the schoolyard fence.

Kaitlin sees the movies
My mom won't let me see.
She remembers the exciting parts
And explains them all to me.

Kaitlin is a wizard
Who brews the strangest stuff
Into magic potions
'Til Mom says, "That's enough."

continued

Katie is my closest friend.
Kaitlin is my favorite, too.
I'm lucky to have two very best friends.
I always have something to do.

Kate, Katie, and Kaitlin are real children who are really friends. Initially, they were drawn to each other because their names were so similar. Over time, they came to appreciate their differences as well as to enjoy the things they had in common.

Toddlers and preschoolers are capable of forming close friendships, and their "best friends" can be particularly important to them. Friends or siblings who play together frequently often develop favorite games, projects, and pretend play scenarios that get more and more elaborate with time. More elaborate often means more opportunities to extend language and literacy, especially when adults support the play by supplying needed props, asking the children about what they are doing, and playing the role of an appreciative audience when asked. In a classroom or family child-care home, intimate spaces such as play lofts, forts, and quiet corners can encourage best friend conversations.

Nicky's Dream

Yesterday Greg and I had fight,
And I pushed him to the floor.
He yelled, "Nick-y, I don't want to be
Your brother any more."

So I yelled back
"I don't care, baby!"
And I really meant it.
I think. Maybe.

Last night I had a scary dream.
It was really, really bad.
At first I thought the dream was true,
Which made me very sad.

I dreamed Greg and I were all alone
And tucked in for the night,
When a man with a purple face came in
And asked, "Want to learn to fight?"

In my dream I said, "No! No! We don't."
But Gregory said, "Show me!"
Then that mean dream man picked my brother up
And dropped him down in the sea.

I screamed, "Help, help!" It woke me up.
I ran to tell my dad.
It was the scariest, awfulest dream
That I had ever had.

I told my dad the story
Though I knew it wasn't true.
He said, "Do you think that scary dream
Was sending a message to you?"

continued

"Maybe the dream was telling me
To be nicer to Greg," I said.
"I think you're right," said Dad. "Good night.
Now go on back to bed."

This morning Gregory jumped on my bed
And I didn't push him away.
Instead I gave him a great big hug
And asked, "What do you want to play?"

When I took Greg to his class at school,
He did something that was really cool.
He said, "Teacher, for share time, I have something to say.
My brother gave me a hug today."

This poem tells a true story of two close-in-age brothers who learned to appreciate each other. Greg was surprised and delighted by the hug Nick gave him. Nick was even more surprised and delighted that Greg valued it enough to brag about it in preschool.

As you share this poem with children, help them follow the story by asking leading but open-ended questions. What does Nicky dream about? What happens to Greg in the dream? Why does Nicky find the dream awful and scary? How does Greg feel when Nicky gives him a hug? How does Nicky feel when Greg tells his teacher about it?

Some children might want to make their own pictures to illustrate the story or work together to make a picture for each verse. They could then retell the story by reading the pictures and their captions. Other children might want to make pictures or picture books of their own dreams.

My Grandmother's Stories

Every single evening, before I go to bed,
My grandma tells me stories that come out of her head.
She tells me many stories about relatives she knew,
And what's best about her stories is that all of them are true.

She tells me about her mother who knew Martin Luther King
And followed him on a freedom walk on a beautiful
day in spring.
She tells me about her children and the great things
they have done.
She put them all through college, every single one.

When Grandma tells me stories, I listen very well.
She has such wondrous things to say, so many things to tell.
And when she tells me stories, her voice is like a song.
It makes me feel all warm inside. I know where I belong.

Every family has stories—and storytellers. Some of the stories are about people who play key roles in a child's life, some are about people who have passed on, and some are about the children themselves. Whether they are funny, or instructive, or just ordinary, these stories help children know who they are and where they come from. From family stories, children learn what matters to the people who matter most to them. They also learn language, rhythms, storytelling patterns, and life lessons that connect them with their families and with their larger heritage. Even quite young children can recognize and cherish the stories that are important to their families. As they grow, they will remember and retell the family stories that were told to them.

The stories you tell young children don't have to be about famous people or important events to make a difference. A recap of the day's events, a memory from your childhood, or an account of something funny or cute that they did as a baby can be special stories to a young child. If you're working with children, be sure to encourage their family members to share these kinds of stories with their children in their home languages.

CHAPTER 4

Fun With Sounds and Words

Young children enjoy learning new words and finding fun ways to share or repeat the words they know. As soon as babies learn to babble, they begin to experiment with sounds. Their babbles get longer and longer, and, before too long, assume the shape of language. Psychologists call it "expressive jargon" because it sounds so much like real language and seems to convey emotion and intent, even though it is only gibberish. As children learn to express themselves with words that others can understand, their use of expressive jargon diminishes.

Still, toddlers and preschoolers enjoy repeating and creating silly words. They memorize nonsense rhymes like "banana fana fo fana" and "acka backa soda cracker." They make up words and combine words in new ways and may repeat phrases that they don't understand just because they like their sound. They remember the words of songs and stories that they like and repeat them over and over again. As their language expands, so does their ability to make up new words and to use their words to ask questions, get information, exchange secrets, share their dreams, and express their desires.

As children's vocabularies enlarge, so does their understanding of how words work. Without being able to say so, they learn that many words have different forms and that some words like *child, is,* and *have* don't follow the regular rules for forming plural or past tense forms. They come to realize that words that sound the same can have different meanings, like *plane* and *plain,* and that the same word can sometimes be used in different ways, like to *dance* a jig or to do a *dance.* They begin to grasp the idea that words can be made up of other words (*sandbox*) and can have prefixes (*nonsense*) or suffixes (*beautiful*), and they develop expectations or guesses about the meaning of these parts when they encounter them in unfamiliar words.

Children who tune into the sounds in their world, to the sounds and syllables that make up words, and to the various forms and uses of the words they know are developing important building blocks for reading.

All Kinds of Days

Some days things are looking up
And other days I'm down.
Some days I am full of smiles
And other days I frown.

Some days I can't find the words
That I would like to say.
On other days I don't need words
I just keep quiet all day.

Research shows that toddlers develop larger vocabularies when their parents and caregivers do a lot of talking with them than they do when the significant adults in their lives are less talkative. Nevertheless, all of us—adults and children alike—have times when we feel like talking and times when we don't.

As we talk with young children, it is important to follow their lead. Sometimes it is difficult to tell whether a child is being quiet because his interest is elsewhere or because he "can't find the words." Sometimes when we comment on what a child is doing or ask her a question whose answer genuinely interests us, we can see the concentration on her face as she thinks about how to respond. Indeed, some educators urge waiting for a full 5 seconds if a young child seems to be trying to formulate a response.

In a noisy environment, it may be hard for children to carry on conversations. One trick for bringing down the noise level is to whisper insistently instead of shouting. If you help children tune in to loud and quiet sounds and practice shouting and then whispering, they can learn to use their "inside voices" when you remind them.

The Words of a Song

Some words stick on the tip of my tongue
Like the words of a song that I have never sung.
And if those words would just fall out,
You would know what I'm singing about.

I sang with the chickadees just this spring.
They always love the songs I sing.
And if my tongue would get out of my way,
I could keep singing songs all day.

Songs are a great way to extend children's vocabularies, encourage play with sounds and words, and teach new languages. When children are first learning a song, you can teach them to hum the words they don't yet know or can't remember. If they like the song and sing it often, the tune, rhythm, and context will help them learn the missing words.

Favorite songs are also a terrific way to direct children's attention to print as they begin to learn to read. You can show children the words in a songbook and point to words as you sing them together, or you can write a favorite song on chart paper and have someone point to the words as a group sings together. Eventually, children will learn to recognize some of the words and will enjoy taking turns with the pointer.

Jeep Ride

We have a jeep
That's very old
It bumps and jumps along.

It jiggles me
On its lumpy seat
As I hum a jumpy song.

Bump, jump, jiggly jump
Bump-ety, jump-ety, bump, bump.
Bump, jump, over the hump
Bump-ety, jump-ety, jump.

This poem tells a true story. The last verse is a song that was composed by a 5-year-old child. She taught it to her 2-year-old brother, and the two sang it together as they rode over bumpy roads in their family's ancient jeep.

The song is easy for young children to learn. They might enjoy pretending to drive and bouncing to the rhythm as they chant it together. You might write the song (final verse) on chart paper, using different colors to highlight the initial letters of *bump, jump,* and *hump.*

You can also use this poem to help children learn the letter J. What J words can they find in the poem? What other J words do they know? Whose names start with a J? Do they know anyone whose name starts with a J sound but is spelled with a different letter?

The Race

We're turning on our racers.
We're ready to begin.
We're revving up our engines,
'Cause we all want to win.

Rrrr-rrrr, rrrr-rrrr, rrrr
Is what our engines say.
Rrrr-rrrr, rrrr-rrrr, rrrr
Our engines roar away.

We rush around the racetrack.
We're racing very fast.
'Cause we all want to come in first
And not to come in last.

Sound effects, such as "*rrr*" for an engine or "beep" for a horn, are among many children's earliest words. Making noises as they "drive" a toy car or push around a miniature truck is an early form of pretend play. Young children who enjoy this kind of play may also enjoy this poem. You may have to help them with some of the vocabulary. What is an engine? What does it mean to "rev" it?

Children who enjoy playing with miniature vehicles or ride-on toys might like to create their own racetracks, with START and FINISH lines, STOP and GO signs, perhaps even a GAS tank.

The poem can also help children to learn the letter R. Although R is a common letter, it can be a bit tricky. The upper- and lowercase forms look quite different. Also, the /r/ sound is difficult for some children to say—or even hear clearly—especially when it comes in the middle of a word. What words can children find in the poem that begin with R? Do they hear the /r/ sound in the middle or near the end of any of the words? Does it help if you exaggerate the /r/ sounds?

Rainy Day Song

Pitter, patter
Pitter, patter
Pitter, patter
Pit.

The rain that pounds
The window pane
Puts polka dots on
It.

Pitter, patter
Pitter, patter
Pitter, patter
Pat.

The rain taps my
Umbrella drum
Just like
That.

This poem can be enjoyed on several levels. Its words are simple and easy to repeat. They capture the sounds and rhythm of rain, and children may enjoy clapping or tapping their legs as they listen to you read it or attempt to say it with you. The poem also tells a story about the rain. Do the children know what polka dots are? Can they draw a picture? What do they think is meant by an "umbrella drum"? What does it sound like?

Children who enjoy this poem might also enjoy exploring the different sounds that rain makes as it strikes different surfaces. You might encourage them to use words like *plop, plink,* and *rat-a-tat* to capture these sounds and to make up similar onomatopoeic words of their own.

Children who are learning letters might enjoy finding all of the Ps in this poem. Ask them to put their hands in front of their mouths as they say some of the P words. Can they feel the "puff" of air? What other words and names do they know that start with a /p/ sound?

Bean Bag Ball

Bean bag ball
We play it in the hall.
You catch a bean bag with your toes
In bean bag ball.

Bean bag ball
We do not let it fall.
Balance the bean bag on your nose
In bean bag ball.

Bean bag ball is a game that anyone can play—either alone or in a group. It can be played with a purchased Hacky Sack or with a homemade "bean bag" stuffed with beans, sand, or rice. The game rules are few and simple, and there are no winners or losers. Children can balance the bags on their noses, toss them in the air and catch them, drop them and try to catch them on their toes, toss or kick them back and forth with a friend, or throw them through a hole in a homemade target.

The fun of the poem, however, is in its tongue-twister title. Can the children say "bean bag ball"? Can they say it three times fast? How do their lips feel after they say it ten times? Children learning their letters might enjoy finding all the words in this poem that begin with B.

Compound Words

Sometimes I like to play with words
By turning them around.
I like them better backside front
They have a nicer sound.

I went into my *roombath*
Just the other night.
I was looking for my *brushtooth*
Which was *whereno* in sight.

I looked under the *clothwash*.
My *brushtooth* wasn't there.
And then I found some *pastetooth*
All over my *brushhair*.

I washed it off with water,
And then I looked some more.
I finally found my *brushtooth*
Up hanging by the door!

I think that words are much more fun
When I *wardsback* turn them.
And so I do a *standhead*
Everwhen I want to learn them.

This poem plays with compound words (and similar expressions that may
be written as two words) by reversing the order of their parts. For younger
children, you might want to read a verse first with the italicized words
arranged conventionally (*bathroom, toothbrush, nowhere,* etc.) and then read
it again with the words turned around. Older children may be able to identify the turned around words themselves and tell you what they are supposed
to be. They might also enjoy coming up with other "*wardsback*" words for
you to turn around.

Mack the Explorer

Mack put his snack
In the pack on his back.
He said, "Bye, Dad.
Bye, Tad.
I'm off to see some things."

Mack saw a rug.
He gave a tug.
What did he see?
A bug in the rug.
He said, "Bye, bug.
Bye, rug.
I'm off to see some things."

Mack saw a swing.
He started to sing.
What did he see?
A ring on the swing.
He said, "Bye, ring.
Bye, swing.
I'm off to see some things."

Mack saw a well.
He started to yell.
What did he see?
A bell in the well.
He said, "Bye, bell.
Bye, well.
I'm off to see some things."

continued

Mack saw a tree.
He counted to three.
What did he see?
A bee in the tree.
He said, "Bye, bee.
Bye, tree.
I'm off to see some things."

Mack saw his dad.
Then he saw Tad.
He said, "Hi, Dad.
Hi, Tad.
I saw a lot of things."

"I saw a bug in a rug
And a ring on a swing,
A bell in a well,
And a bee in a tree.
Then I saw you,
And now you see me!"

This poem was written for beginning readers, but it is also fun for children who are not yet reading on their own. It has a strong repeating pattern that many children will pick up along with the simple rhymes. This makes it easy to learn and also makes it easy for children and adults to add new verses of their own.

Some children might like to make books of Mack's adventures, using the poem's words or their own, and then read them back to their parents, dolls, or younger siblings.

When children begin to read "for real," they will learn that letters and letter combinations represent the sounds that make up words. They will learn to recognize the letters that represent beginning sounds, or onsets, and the combinations of letters that represent common syllable endings, or "rimes." Learning to recognize common combinations like *-ack, -og,* and *-ing* is generally easier than learning each letter and its sound separately.

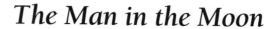

The Man in the Moon

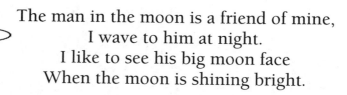

The man in the moon is a friend of mine,
I wave to him at night.
I like to see his big moon face
When the moon is shining bright.

The man in the moon has a crooked smile
That makes me smile, too.
If you make a face and wink your eye,
He'll wink back at you.

The man in the moon has a marshmallow nose
That's soft and puffy and white.
He has no teeth but he likes sweets,
So he munches with his mouth shut tight.

The man in the moon makes a mean, mad face
When the clouds get in his eyes.
Then he makes them go with a mighty blow,
'Cause he is so very wise.

This playful poem can be enjoyed for sheer silliness and word play. As you share it repeatedly with children, encourage them to learn some of the lines or words and say them along with you. You might want to pause before the last word of each stanza and see if the children can fill in the word themselves.

Children who get interested in "the man in the moon" might like to explore further. Find some pictures of the moon in different phases. Can children see the "man" in the patterns of the craters? Encourage them to look at the real moon at night, draw pictures of what they see, and then look at the moon on another night and compare it with the pictures they drew.

Children who are showing an interest in letters and their sounds might enjoy finding some of the Ms in this poem. The letter M is often one of the first letters that children learn to recognize: its sound is easy to say and easy to elongate or exaggerate, its two bumps are easy to recognize, its upper and lowercase forms are similar, and it is found in common logos like McDonald's and M&Ms.

Word Puzzles

How can I go to sleep at night?
How can I go to bed,
When oh so many puzzling things
Are tumbling through my head?

Today turns into yesterday,
And here turns into there.
Tomorrow never comes at all—
I do not think it's fair.

Some children develop a fascination with words very early. They prefer big words like *turquoise, front loader, delicious,* and *adorable* to simpler ones like *blue, truck, good,* and *cute.* They enjoy matching opposites or synonyms, and they love riddles and puns that turn on multiple meanings of the same or similar words. They wonder about the meanings, sounds, and uses of new words that they hear, and may even ask questions about words that are familiar.

As you share this poem with children, talk with them about what they think the second verse means. How does *today* turn into *yesterday*? How does *here* become *there*? (You might show them how the *t* is added, as well as talking about what happens when you move from one place to another.) Why doesn't *tomorrow* ever come?

You might also ask children to tell you what *they* wonder about. Whatever it is, it is likely to be surprising. One family added question time to their children's bedtime routine and was delighted to hear questions like "Where did dinosaurs choose to lay their eggs?" "What is outside of the universe?" and "What does *supercalifragilisticexpialidocious* mean?"

Rhymes

Rhymes are words that sound alike
Like stumble and grumble, hike and bike

Potatoes, tomatoes, collars and hollers
Invite, delight, scholars and dollars

Fishes, dishes, yellow and fellow
Parading, trading, mellow and Jell-O

Toaster, boaster, scatter and chatter
Rooster, booster, matter and clatter

Funny, honey, baker and maker
Cozy, rosy, taker and shaker

Heater, beater, butter and mutter
Daisy, lazy, shutter and putter

Dragon, wagon, shoulder and bolder
Happy, scrappy, older and bolder

Heaven, seven, hog and log
Cleaner, meaner, dog and frog

Gobble, hobble, creamer and streamer
Cable, able, schemer and beamer

Handle, candle, pewter and cuter
Fairy, hairy, tutor and suitor

Marry, carry, puddle and muddle
Beginning, winning, huddle and cuddle

Dozing, posing, seating and eating
Rhyming, timing, meeting, repeating

continued

Vacation, creation, stamper and damper
Flowering, showering, hamper and camper

Hotel, motel, zipper and ripper
Shouting, pouting, dipper and slipper

Candy, handy, lending and tending
Relaxing, faxing, spending and ending.

Rhymes can be longer than one syllable, as this poem full of two and three syllable rhymes demonstrates. Children who enjoy rhymes may like poems like this, even when they don't know what some of the words mean. They may also enjoy learning the meanings of the new words and making (and perhaps also illustrating) their own collections of rhymes.

My Favorite Things

Acorns, artichokes, asparagus, and arks.
Banjos, bakeries, baseball, and barks.

Cabbage, cauliflower, cottages, and cabs.
Dollars, donkeys, dribbles, and dabs.

Escalators, easels, elephants, and etchers.
Faces, flamingos, farmhouses, and fetchers.

Gorillas, garbage trucks, garlic bread, and ghosts.
Hamburgers, hopscotch, harnesses, and hosts.

Igloos, iguanas, ice cream, and iced teas.
Jokers, jellybeans, jazz, and jamborees.

Kittens, koala bears, kangaroos, and kites.
Leopards, lollipops, licorice, and lights.

Motorcycles, monkeys, marshmallows, and moats.
Nature trails, noses, nurseries, and notes.

Orchids, ostriches, operas, and otters.
Pumpkins, puddles, parasols, and potters.

Questions, quackers, queen bees, and quinces.
Raindrops, riding boots, and really red rinses.

Sardines, submarines, saxophones, and sacks.
Taxis, tournaments, tambourines, and tacks.

Underwear, umbrellas, ukeleles, and Undo.
Violets, Virginia, Velcro, and a view.

continued

Watermelon, windmills, watches, and wham.
X-box, xylophone, x-ray, and exam.

Yo-yos, yellow bows, yodeling, and you.
Zebras, zinnias, zippers, and the zoo.

As you share this poem with children, you might talk with them about their favorite things. What foods, toys, animals, and colors do they like best? Do they like special places, games, or activities? Is there something that they've read about in books that they wish they could see? Do they like certain words?

Some children might like to make collections of their favorite things (or people or words). They can search for pictures in magazines and catalogs or draw pictures of their own. An easy and fun project for little ones is to make a mobile by pasting pictures of favorite things onto cardboard cutouts, punching a hole in each cutout, and hanging them with strings from a coat hanger or dowel. You can write or paste a label on the back of each item.

Some children might like to collect pictures of things that start with the first letter of their names or make their own *ABC* books.

Vocabulary

Apatasaurus was a big dinosaur
Who ate all the plants and wanted some more.

Baffling is something you can't figure out
What is this *baffling* poem about?

A *chameleon* is a lizard that changes its skin
To the color of the place that it finds itself in.

A *daring* person is very brave
When there's a tiger that she needs to save.

Elegant means looking fancy and fine.
You look elegant in that dress of mine.

Famished means so hungry that you could eat
Enough dinner for two and still want a treat.

Galloping is the way that horses run.
I always think that it looks like fun.

Humongous means really, really big—
As big as a house or an oil rig.

Imitation is what people do
When they try to copy you.

Jovial means happy and gay.
I like it when I feel that way.

Kin is someone related to you.
I hope you like her as much as I do.

A *limousine* is a taxi that's very expensive.
It's fancy inside and its size is extensive.

continued

Miniature is teeny teeny tiny.
My *miniature* cars are very shiny.

Noxious is awful, like a terrible smell.
When something smells *noxious* you really can tell.

An *orphan* is someone who has no mom or dad—
No parents to tell her she's been good or bad.

A *pansy* is a flower that looks like a face.
In my garden we have them all over the place.

A *quarrel* is a fight you have with your brother
When you just won't listen to each other.

Ridiculous means silly and crazy and dumb—
Like wearing your shoe on the end of your thumb.

Slither means to slide like a long, wiggly snake
That sneaks through the grass before you're awake.

Tedious means boring and taking too long,
Like a task that's too hard cause you're doing it wrong.

A *unicorn* is a magical one-horned horse
That's only found in books, of course.

A *vibrant* color is very bright.
It shines and shimmers in the light.

Wasteful is something you should not be,
Like those people in Boston who threw out the tea.

An *exit* is a way to get out
Of a crowded room or a roundabout.

A *yardstick* is something that you use to measure
How tall you have grown or the size of a treasure.

continued

A *zither* is an instrument with strings you can strum
As you play favorite songs that you like to hum.

We wrote this poem for small children who love big words. As you share it with children, talk with them about any words that they did not know before. Use them in sentences yourself, and work with the children to find pictures that illustrate their meanings. Help the children find more opportunities to use the new words. You might also ask the children to talk about the longest word that they know. What does it mean? Can they use it in a sentence?

CHAPTER 5

Pets and Other Animals

M ost young children are fascinated with animals. Even children who are afraid of the dogs and cats in their neighborhood, or of the larger animals in the zoo or in their story books, are likely to be curious about how animals behave and what they might be thinking or feeling. They are likely to ask questions about where animals sleep, what they do when it rains, and how they take care of their babies.

Of course, young children's ideas about animals are usually mixed with fantasy. They see pets as members of the family and may want to treat them as siblings or playmates—whether or not the pet is interested. Likewise, their stuffed animals are often given human personalities and characteristics. Their storybooks are filled with animal characters that represent human feelings and relationships. Indeed, when an issue like fears or misbehavior or jealousy hits close to home, it is often easier for children to talk about how animal characters deal with the problem than to talk about how people deal with it.

Although we would not want to take away children's fantasies, it is important to provide them with real information as well. Children need access to lots of nonfiction as well as fiction books, even if they are only looking at pictures or naming the animals or making their sounds. As their interests develop further, they can learn about the needs of pets and other animals and become "experts" on their care.

The poems in this collection build on children's interests. Some are realistic; others are quite fanciful. All, however, provide opportunities for children to learn more about animals and their environments—and to pick up related vocabulary and concepts.

Caring for Pets

I take care of the pets I own.
I always give my dog a bone.
When he wants to go, I take him out,
And then I let him run about.

I take good care of my kitten, too.
I pet her when she starts to mew.
She likes to chase my rubber ball
When I roll it down the hall.

I also take good care of my birds.
I taught my parrot lots of words.
And when my friends come over to play,
My parrot knows what words to say.

The child in this poem is lucky to have several pets, and she has learned a lot about their needs. Of course, we wouldn't expect her to be consistent in her care or to remember to see things from the pet's point of view. Still, she has a lot of "expert" knowledge that she can share with classmates and friends.

Many children who have pets consider them to be family members. They wouldn't dream of drawing a family picture without including the pet(s). They may enjoy making their pets birthday cards or small presents, making books about them, or even making books for them and reading them the story.

Children who don't have real pets may have imaginary friends, miniature toys, or stuffed animals that can play the same role. They may enjoy sharing them with classmates and making up stories about them.

My Puppy

My puppy always likes to cuddle.
She thinks she is a queen.
And so I put her in a puddle
To get her nice and clean.

My puppy has a wiggly tail.
It wiggles all day long.
She tries to tinkle in the pail
But often gets it wrong.

Baby animals are especially appealing to young children. You may want to
join them in baby animal play. You can try moving like the animals, guess-
ing which animal someone is pretending to be, or using toy animals like
puppets and playing out stories of eating, sleeping, going places, or getting
lost and then being found. As you play together, you can introduce baby
animal names like *cub, foal, calf,* and *duckling* and verbs like *fetch, yip, purr,
amble, gallop,* and *nuzzle.*

Playing Together

I am so very lucky.
I have a little pup
Who licks my face and plays with me
As soon as I get up.

Whenever I throw a ball to her,
She brings it back to me.
One day I threw it much too high.
Its catcher was a tree.

My Little Inchworm

I have a little inchworm
That lives inside a box.
It inches over mud and sticks
And wiggles over rocks.

I feed my little inchworm
Some bits of leaf for lunch.
He seems to take such tiny bites
I think I hear him munch.

I watch my little inchworm
Is my inchworm watching me?
I think that maybe now it's time
To set my inchworm free.

An inchworm gets its name from its size—it is about an inch long. But its name also describes its behavior; it inches along a stick, stretching out full length and then bringing its hind end up to its front and then stretching out again, as if it is trying to measure the stick.

Children might enjoy searching for inchworms or similar-sized creatures like earthworms, caterpillars, or centipedes. Before beginning the hunt, show them how big an inch is. Some children might enjoy just watching the creepy crawlers they discover; others will insist on feeding them, measuring them, or taking them home to keep as pets. You can use the poem to help children remember that most wild animals—even tiny ones—are happiest in their own homes.

For children who are learning letters, this poem can be a helpful way of remembering the letter I. Children might think of it as an inchworm that is standing up very straight.

The letter I can be tricky because, like other vowels, it has both long and short sounds. It is a word in its own right and its name and long sound sound like the word *eye*. Yet common words like *it*, *itchy*, *if*, and *inchworm* begin with the short /i /sound. Children who like the poem might enjoy finding some of the I words in it. In which words does I say its name? In which words does I have a different sound?

Pets and Other Animals • **79**

Tommy Turtle

Tommy Turtle tickles me
With his tiny toes.
But if I try to tickle him—
In his shell he goes.

Tommy likes to take a swim
Till he tires of his play.
He sits on top of his tippy rock
And sleeps the day away.

Once upon a time, turtles were popular classroom pets. Unfortunately, they can carry salmonella, so now most children encounter them only in books, zoos, or aquariums.

This poem is fun to act out with children. Ask a child to put out his hand. Make a fist, tell him it is your "turtle," and place it on his open hand. As you recite the first verse of the poem, tickle his palm with your fingernails, then quickly close your fist as the turtle goes into its shell. Children will enjoy taking the role of the turtle, either using their own two hands or tickling a friend.

The first line of the poem is also fun to say as a tongue twister. How quickly can children say it? Children who are learning their letters can have fun finding all of the words in this poem that start with T.

My Hamster

I have a happy hamster.
He always loves to play.
He did some very clever tricks
The day before yesterday.

He made his cage jump up and down,
And then he tried to sit.
I laughed so hard when I watched him
I almost had a fit.

Hamsters (and gerbils) make great classroom pets because their antics are so much fun to watch. A class pet also provides many opportunities to support emergent literacy—without the children even realizing it. Children can make a nametag for the pet's cage and a sign that invites visitors to view their new pet, tells them he likes to be watched and talked to, or warns them that he doesn't like to be picked up. They can teach each other to follow simple, written instructions for daily feeding (you can use rebuses to show how many spoonfuls of food to give and to remind them to refill the water bottle.) The children can follow a simple chart that tells whose turn it is to feed the pet or clean the cage. In the process, they are likely to learn to recognize their own and each other's names, as well, of course, as the name of their pet.

Sammy the Seal

Sammy sat upon the mat.
He sat and sat and sat.
Sally said, "Silly Sammy.
Don't just sit like that."

See Sammy swim.
See Sammy slide.
Sammy sings a seal-y song
And gives his ball a ride.

In case you can't tell, Sammy is a performing seal and Sally is his trainer. Children may enjoy acting out this poem, with a narrator reading most of the poem, Sally telling Sammy what to do, and Sammy swimming, sliding back onto the stage, barking, and balancing a ball on his nose as the narrator and Sally cue him.

For children who are interested in letters and or are beginning to decode words, this poem also provides an opportunity to find lots of Ss (an easy first letter to learn because of its distinctive shape and easily elongated sound) and to read simple words like *sit, sat,* and *mat* in a meaningful context.

Fiona the Farmer

Fiona, the farmer, didn't want any harm
To come to the pig that she kept on her farm.
She put up a fence and a fine, fancy wall
At the edge of the barn by her horse's new stall.

When the horse saw the pigsty, he started to neigh
"That pig will smell funny, and get in my way."
Then the pig stamped his feet and turned up his nose
"That horse leaves a stink wherever he goes."

So Fiona filled up the pigsty with flowers.
The pig found them fragrant and sniffed them for hours.
The horse stopped his fussing and savored the smell,
So Fiona, the farmer, was happy as well.

For children who love farm animals, here's a fanciful poem about a farmer who pays attention to her animals' needs, quirks, and desires. The poem also introduces some vocabulary that may be new to young children: *barn, stall, pigsty, fragrant, sniff,* and *savor.* Children who enjoy the poem might like to make a miniature farm with blocks or other toys and rubber animals. As you talk together about what their animals want and need, you can practice some of these new words and introduce others.

Where Animals Sleep

Most animals go to sleep at night
In a place that's out of sight.
If the animal is a bear,
She'll go to sleep inside a lair.

If the animal is a sheep,
He will probably go to sleep
Inside a barn on a bed of hay.
He might even sleep there during the day.

If the animal is a bird,
She'll sleep in a nest, or so I've heard.
That nest made of twigs is likely to be
Way up high on the branch of a tree.

If the animal is a cat,
He will probably sleep on a mat.
And sometimes he will sleep on a bed
Beside his favorite sleepy head.

If the animal is a baby kangaroo,
I think I know what she would do.
She will sleep in her mother's pouch,
Pretending that it is a couch.

If the animal is a bat,
He'll go to sleep wherever he's at.
Bats fly all night and sleep all day.
A cave is where they like to stay.

continued

A turtle, as you know quite well,
Goes to sleep inside her shell.
I think she goes to sleep at night,
But I'm not sure that I am right.

Children who love animals often wonder where they sleep at night and worry about whether they will be safe and comfortable. This poem just begins to answer their questions. Encourage interested children to explore further. Find picture books, nature guides, and even books for older children that show animal homes. When you take children on outings, look for anthills, bird's nests, and holes where snakes, chipmunks, or rabbits might live. You can also look for large bundles of twigs high in trees where squirrels live in their nests.

My Cat Funny

My cat is fine and furry.
She has a funny face.
She's always in a hurry
To finish every race.

Her fur is soft and fluffy,
Which makes her look quite fat.
She gets all round and puffy
When she gets into a spat.

My funny cat has double paws.
Each front foot has ten toes!
We hear the clicking of her claws
Everywhere she goes.

She offers me torn flowers
Before she takes her nap.
And she spends many hours
Purring softly in my lap.

Funny was a Maine Coon cat with long hair who belonged to friends of ours. Some members of this breed (and others) are referred to as "mitten cats" because they have extra toes or "double paws" that make their feet look very wide, as if they are wearing mittens. Funny had some extra toes on both her front and back feet, with ten toes on each front foot.

Children who have pets might enjoy drawing pictures of them and making lists of their special characteristics. What is the pet's name? What kind of animal is it? What does it look like? What does it like to do? Where does it sleep? Does it do any tricks? What other special things does it do that make them laugh?

Children who are learning their letters might enjoy making a "fighting cat" sound—"ffff!!" They can also have fun finding all the F words in the poem. Do they know any people whose names start with F, or whose names begin with a /f/ sound that is written as Ph?

Edgar the Egret

Edgar the Egret had a snowy white feather
That tickled his nose in bad stormy weather.
One day, at sunrise, he spotted some sun
And told his mate She-gret, "Let's go have fun."

They escaped from the Everglades and flew to
the ocean
Where they encountered some seagulls making
quite a commotion
Chasing pelicans and ospreys in the cool ocean breezes.
But Edgar and She-gret couldn't stifle their sneezes.

They flew back to their nest for a much needed rest
And decided that eating at home would be best.
Their friend the flamingo stood and watched on one leg
As She-gret the Egret laid a lovely white egg.

This poem mixes real information with fantasy. Egrets are snowy white birds that live in marshy places throughout the world. They are quite common in the Florida Everglades, a "river of grass" that runs through the center of the southern part of the state. In southern Florida, the Everglades are not far from the ocean, where seagulls, pelicans, and ospreys abound. Egrets lay white eggs in nests that they build in trees high above the ground or in marshes and reeds over the water, but they probably do not sneeze.

Children might enjoy looking up some of the birds in this poem in guidebooks or on the Internet. They might also like to create a mural showing animals that live in the Everglades or in an area that they have visited. Children paint a simple background—land, sky, and perhaps water, tall grass, or a tree—on a large sheet of paper. Each child can then draw and cut out pictures, or cut them from magazines, and place them on the mural. To enhance the literacy value, create a key listing all of the animals. Encourage children to point them out as they give "tours" of their mural. Help them find the names on the list.

Children learning letters can find **E**s in this poem. They may notice that even in Edgar the Egret's name, **E** can stand for different sounds.

The Otter and the Octopus

The otter and the octopus
Were frolicking in the sea.
The octopus asked the otter
"Would you like to dance with me?"

"OK," said the otter,
Overcome by Octy's charms.
But though he was sold,
He just couldn't hold
All of those octopus arms.

Then the otter showed the octopus
How to curl up and touch her nose.
So they frolicked away
That whole long day
Making lots and lots of Os.

It is doubtful that a sea otter ever danced with an octopus, though both animals can be found in the northern Pacific Ocean and are about the same size. The North Pacific octopus, the largest octopus in the world, can grow to be more than 30 feet long and weigh more than 100 pounds. Sea otters spend a lot of time floating on their backs and are very graceful underwater. Both otters and octopi can make circles with their bodies.

In addition to *otter* and *octopus*, this poem introduces other vocabulary that may be new to children: *frolic, overcome,* and an unusual use of the common word *sold*. You'll notice that all of these words contain either the long or short /o/ sound. Children who are learning their letters might like to find the Os in the poem, look for Os in their own and their friends' names, or make ocean pictures and fill them with things that start with, contain, or look like Os.

Goats

If you are wearing your favorite coat,
Do not get anywhere near a goat.
You know that goats like to eat
Anything they happen to meet.

One day I came across a goat
Chewing a coat that got stuck in his throat.
He choked and coughed and pranced all about,
But the coat in his throat just would not come out.

Goats are notoriously unfussy eaters and have been known to swallow strange objects. Usually, though, they prefer grasses and grains. As you share this poem with children, talk with them about their experiences with goats or about your own experiences. Have any of you ever seen a goat? How did it behave? Have you ever tasted goat cheese or goat's milk? Have you ever seen a herd of wild goats or a goat farm?

Goats are found all over the world and provide food for many people. Children will enjoy learning about goat herders and tasting ethnic foods made from goat milk or meat.

Little Cat's Big Dreams

I'm just a little cat
Sleeping on a mat.
What's so good about that?

If I were a lion,
I'd nap in the sun.
And then I'd leap and run
And have so much fun.

I dream I am a tiger
With stripes on my side
And a mouth that opens wide
With big teeth inside.

I dream I am a leopard
With lots and lots and lots
And lots of dots.
I like my spots.

I dream I am a cheetah.
I chase and chase and chase
And win the race
To my secret place.

But then my person pets me
And I open up my eyes.
She says, to my surprise:

"I don't want a lion or a tiger for a pet.
A leopard or a cheetah is not what I will get.
Those big wild cats belong in a zoo.
I'll take you."

continued

I'm a happy little cat
Sitting on my mat.
And I like that.

Children who like this poem may enjoy finding out more about big cats. Help them discover an interesting fact about each one: how fast a cheetah can run, how big a tiger can grow, where leopards live or how many are left in the world, or the differences in behavior between male and female lions. Can they identify pictures of different kinds of big cats? How are these cats alike? How are they different?

Camels

Would you like to learn about a camel?
He is, you know, my favorite mammal.
A dromedary camel is one-humped,
And if you ride on him you will get bumped.

A camel is special in many ways.
He can walk through the desert for days upon days.
He carries water in his inside.
That's why he can take you on such a long ride.

Camels can teach you quite a lot
About staying cool when you are hot.
So when you feel the temperature rise,
Keep yourself cool and open your eyes.

Camels are always very kind.
If you are sulky, they do not mind.
A camel will show you how to smile,
And then you'll stay happy for quite awhile.

A camel depends on his own resources.
He keeps to the path whatever the course is.
And you can make your dreams come true
By doing what the camels do.

It has been said that camels were designed by a committee. Their appearance is unusual, but they are perfectly suited to their desert environment. Their large feet keep them from sinking in the sand and their fatty humps store energy so they can go for many days without eating. Many people think that the humps "carry" water, but this is not quite right. A camel can drink a large amount of water at a time, which is stored in its bloodstream. Thus camels can go for several days without drinking.

continued

Because of these qualities, we think of camels as both adaptable and resourceful. They are able to solve their own problems by planning ahead and by drawing upon their inner strengths and special abilities. They keep going even when the going is rough.

By encouraging children to try things themselves, to use their words to talk through a problem, and to look for a different approach if the one they are trying doesn't seem to be working, we help them to be resourceful, adaptable learners. When we talk, read, and play with them in ways that build their vocabularies, we give them a store of words that can see them through the long, exciting journey into literacy.

CHAPTER
6

New Twists on Old Favorites

S illy songs, movement games, and finger plays are the stock in trade of toddler and preschool programs. They entertain children, engage them in a group activity, and provide them with opportunities to learn new skills that they can show off to an appreciative audience of parents or grandparents. At the same time, these traditional songs and games provide wonderful opportunities to support language, content learning, and emergent literacy.

With their rollicking rhythms, simple rhymes, and repeated elements, traditional preschool songs and chants are fun to recite and memorize. Accompanying actions enable children to participate, even if they can't say or don't know the words, and help them to keep track of the sequence. Writing the words to children's favorites on large chart paper as an additional cue can help them associate written with spoken words. When most of the words are repeated (as in *Old MacDonald Had a Farm*), you can accompany the words that change with each line or verse with a picture clue. Before you know it, children will be reading the words as they sing along.

Another wonderful aspect of traditional children's favorites is that they lend themselves to variation. Children who like to play with words can make up their own variants—the sillier the better—and exercise their oral memories and phonological awareness (tuning in to sounds, especially those that make up words) at the same time. Adults can also create variants that incorporate new vocabulary or call attention to particular sounds. These provide fun ways for children to practice new knowledge and skills in a familiar context. They also inspire children to create new verses of their own. Reading teachers call this "innovation on text" and recommend it as a technique for practicing reading and writing as well as for oral language play.

Traditional songs and movement games, or their variants, can be used to accompany and enhance routines ("This is the way we pick up the blocks"), to teach basic concepts and vocabulary ("Put your right arm in, put your right arm out"), and to help children get to know and appreciate each other ("Hello, Rosa, yes indeed. . . . Yes indeed, my darling"). Finger plays are especially good for practicing counting and for developing the muscles and coordination needed for writing.

Children who enjoy both the traditional version of a chant or song and a new twist that they learned or helped create may be inspired to teach these verses to others. Some children might even want to make songbooks, adding their own illustrations to words that an adult records or helps them write.

To get children and the adults who teach and play with them started on a limitless source of entertainment, invention, and learning, we offer a few of our own new twists on old favorites.

Old MacDonald Had a Swamp

Old MacDonald had a swamp
E-I-E-I-O.
And in his swamp he had an alligator.
E-I-E-I-O.
With a chomp-chomp here
And a chomp-chomp there.
Here a chomp. There a chomp.
Everywhere a chomp-chomp.
Old MacDonald had a swamp
E-I-E-I-O.

Old MacDonald had a swamp
E-I-E-I-O.
And in his swamp he had frog.
E-I-E-I-O.
With a ribbet-ribbet here
And a ribbet-ribbet there.
Here a ribbet. There a ribbet.
Everywhere a ribbet-ribbet.
Old MacDonald had a swamp
E-I-E-I-O.

Depending on the kind of swamp you are envisioning, you may want to add a snapping turtle (snap-snap), some reeds (swish-swish), a beaver (slap-slap), some crickets (chirp-chirp), some mud (slurp-slurp), a catfish (glub-glub), some geese (honk-honk), a water snake (hiss-hiss), or a rowboat (splash-splash).

Of course, Old MacDonald's possessions can extend beyond a farm and a swamp. He (or one of his friends) could have a circus, a zoo, a road, a gas station, an orchestra, or even a birthday party. The possibilities are limitless. Children who have been studying a particular area might want to incorporate their knowledge of the items that are found there, and the sounds associated with them, into a new twist on *Old MacDonald*.

She'll Be Comin' 'Round the Kitchen

She'll be comin' 'round the kitchen when she comes.
She'll be comin' 'round the kitchen when she comes.
She'll be comin' 'round the kitchen
When her panties need some stitchin'.
She'll be comin' 'round the kitchen when she comes.

She'll be plantin' some nice flowers when she comes.
She'll be plantin' some nice flowers when she comes.
When the cold north wind's a-blowin'
And there is nothing that is growin'.
She'll be plantin' some nice flowers when she comes.

She'll be eatin' mashed potatoes when she comes.
She'll be eatin' mashed potatoes when she comes.
She'll be eatin' mashed potatoes
While she's suckin' on tomatoes.
She'll be eatin' mashed potatoes when she comes.

Adding verses to this song can be a group effort. You can challenge children to think of things that the woman in the poem who is "comin'" might be doing, see if anyone can come up with a rhyming word, and then use rhymes to create the lines. You might begin with a theme, such as all the things she might be riding on, food she might be bringing, or instruments she might be playing. Remember, it's perfectly fine to use nonsense words or to put in lines that don't make any sense. As long as the children have contributed, they are likely to be happy with the result.

If You're Angry and You Know It

If you're angry and you know it, take a breath.
If you're angry and you know it, take a breath.
If you're angry and you know it,
then you're face will surely show it.
If you're angry and you know it, take a breath.

If you're proud and you know it, stand up tall.
If you're proud and you know it, stand up tall.
If you're proud and you know it,
then your face will surely show it.
If you're proud and you know it, stand up tall.

As children mature from babies to toddlers to preschoolers, they learn to express a wider and wider range of feelings and to recognize them in others. Tuning into their own and others' feelings helps children find appropriate ways of expressing themselves and responding to others. It helps them to stay in control when they are excited, elated, angry, or upset; to consider others' needs as well as their own; to take appropriate actions to make themselves feel better; and to ask for help when they need it.

After introducing children to this extension of *When You're Happy and You Know It,* talk with them about other ways that they might feel, and how they would know that they or others are feeling that way. What do they do when they're feeling grumpy? silly? sleepy? What would be a good thing to do if they're feeling lonesome? hungry? scared?

The Trees Are Growing Tall

The trees are growing tall.
The trees are growing tall.
With soil and rain and sunny days
The trees are growing tall.

The trees are growing roots.
The trees are growing roots.
With soil and rain and sunny days
The trees are growing roots.

The trees are growing bark.
The trees are growing bark.
With soil and rain and sunny days
The trees are growing bark.

The trees are growing leaves.
The trees are growing leaves.
With soil and rain and sunny days
The trees are growing leaves.

Sing this song to the tune of "The Farmer in the Dell." It was written by Carol Anastas, a teacher at the Family Center Preschool at Nova Southeastern University for her 3-year-old class. Ms. Carol wrote the song on a large piece of chart paper and illustrated the key words with pictures of trees and tree roots, a real piece of bark, and a cluster of leaves. The children soon learned to read the words as they sang the song together.

As they learn more about growing plants, the children construct new variants of the song. They sing about the vegetables in their garden ("The tomatoes are turning red...The peppers are getting ripe") and about the Great Kapok Tree that provides homes for rainforest animals in the book they are reading together ("The kapok tree grows tall...The monkeys swing in its branches").

The Blade on the Bulldozer

The blade on the bulldozer goes
Push-push-push. Push-push-push. Push-push-push.
The blade on the bulldozer goes
Push-push-push
All around the construction site.

The bucket on the front loader goes
Scoop-scoop-scoop. Scoop-scoop-scoop. Scoop-scoop-scoop.
The bucket on the front loader goes
Scoop-scoop-scoop
All around the construction site.

The bed on the dump truck
Dumps its load. Dumps its load. Dumps its load.
The bed on the dump truck dumps its load
All around the construction site.

The safety engineer says
"Wear your hard hat. Wear your hard hat. Wear your hard hat."
The safety engineer says
"Wear your hard hat"
All around the construction site.

Creating a variant of *The Wheels on the Bus* is a wonderful way to keep children busy on the way back from a field trip and to help them tell the story of their adventure. Children who have been to an airport, grocery store, bank, petting zoo, or fire station will have heard and seen lots of things. Putting them into a song will help them to remember the experience and practice any new vocabulary.

Little Boy Blue

Little Boy Blue
Come blow your horn.
The sheep are eating up
All of the corn.

The wind is blowing.
The sheep are all cold.
And none of the sheep
Will do what they are told.

The nursery rhymes that we had memorized as young children and have
passed down to our children are fun to say, but often seem nonsensical, violent, inappropriate, or out of date if we stop to analyze the words. Nevertheless, they are an important part of every culture. They give children good
practice with rhyme and rhythm, help them tune into the sounds that make
up words, and can be soothing to children who have heard them often. It
can be fun to make up new versions.

Row, Row, Row Your Boat

Row, row, row your boat
Gently down the stream.
Merrily, merrily, merrily, merrily—
Life is but a dream.

Scoot, scoot, scoot your scooter
All around the room.
Zippity, zippity, zippity, zippity
Zippity, zippity, zoom.

Ride, ride, ride your zebra
All around the zoo.
Galloping, galloping, galloping, galloping—
It's such fun for you.

Zip, zip, zip your zipper.
Zip and do not stop.
Pull it up, pull it up, pull it up, pull it up—
Until you reach the top.

Read, read, read your book.
Read it with a friend.
Breeze along, breeze along, breeze along, breeze along—
Until you reach THE END.

Row, Row, Row Your Boat is a great song to use with babies and toddlers. They can exercise their abdominal muscles as they hold your hands and rock back and forth. This variant can be fun for toddlers and preschoolers to act out. It's also a great source of **Z** words for children who are learning their letters.

Nursery Rhymes

Have you heard about the crazy cow
Who jumped over the moon? Don't ask me how.
The dish and the spoon ran away with each other
Without permission from their mother.

Do you remember when Jack and Jill
Chased each other up a very big hill?
Did you know Humpty Dumpty at all?
He made a big splat when he fell off a wall.

Do you remember the pumpkin eater?
He is very skinny and his name is Peter.
Do you remember Jack, who was nimble and quick?
I don't know why he jumped over a candlestick.

Did you know Mary, who was quite contrary?
Her feet were enormous and her head was quite hairy.
When someone told her to go away
She said, "I will not. I am here to stay."

Did you know the old woman who lived in a shoe
And had so many children she didn't know what to do?
She gave them some broth without any bread.
She should have given them ice cream instead.

Do you remember Little Jack Horner?
He ate pumpkin pie when he sat in his corner.
Before he swallowed his last bite of pie
He sneezed and the pumpkin blew into his eye.

Do you remember Little Miss Muffet
Who liked eating lunch while she sat on a tuffet?
When a spider tried to share her seat,
Miss Muffet jumped up onto her feet.

continued

Do you remember Simple Simon
Who went to the county fair?
The fair was the funniest show in town
I wish that I had been there.

Children and grown-ups who like Mother Goose rhymes may enjoy these updated commentaries. Can children recite the rhymes they are based on? If not, would they like to learn them?

Alice in Wonderland

Have you ever heard of a Cheshire cat
Do you ever wonder where he is at?
He has found a place that is really grand
He is waiting for Alice in Wonderland.

I Made a Mistake

I woke up in the morning and I jumped out of bed.
I made a mistake and I bumped my head.

I went to the closet to put on my pants.
I made a mistake and I put on my plants.

I went to the dresser to put on my shirt.
I made a mistake and I put on some dirt.

I went to the bathroom to brush my hair.
I made a mistake and I brushed my bear.

I went to the door to let out the dog.
I made a mistake and I let in a frog.

I went to the kitchen to bake a waffle.
I made a mistake and it smelled awful.

I went to my bedroom and I counted to ten.
I jumped into bed and I started again.

The first verse of this poem comes from a traditional jump rope rhyme.
We've added some silly verses of our own just for fun. Children may enjoy
extending the pattern, especially if you give them a first line.

Jump rope rhymes and hand-clapping games from many cultures reflect
children's creativity and enjoyment of word play. Ask parents and grandparents to help you make a multicultural collection, and encourage children to
add their own silly words.

One Little Garbage Truck

One little garbage truck had lots of things to do.
He honked his horn, and then there were two.
Two little garbage trucks were busy as could be.
They called for a friend, and then there were three.

Three little garbage trucks loading up some more
Filled up their bins, then flagged down truck four.
Four little garbage trucks going down the drive
Reached their destination—and found truck number five.

Five little garbage trucks picking up the trash—
One went through a red light, and there was a crash.
Four little garbage trucks driving through the muck—
One skidded through a puddle, and then he got stuck.

Three little garbage trucks, rolling through the mire—
One picked up a nail, and got a flat tire.
Two little garbage trucks crawling through the mud—
One hit a tree trunk—with a very loud thud.

One little garbage truck, finished for the day,
Started to go home, but then went the wrong way.
No little garbage trucks rumbling down the roads—
Tomorrow they'll go out again to gather up their loads.

This variant on *One Little Pumpkin* (and endless similar finger plays) gives children who like trucks practice in counting forward and backward. Have them hold up the appropriate number of fingers as they listen to or say each verse.

Reading

I always like to read a story
With my big sister, whose name is Kori.
When Kori reads a story, I have to smile,
And she likes to read to me once in a while.

She read me a book that I never knew
About Christopher Robin and Winnie the Pooh.
When Tigger started bouncing, he bounced so high
That he nearly almost got lost in the sky.

Then she read about rabbit and his relations.
All of them had good imaginations.
And then she told me that Kanga, too,
Had a jumpy baby whose name was Roo.

Eeyore, the donkey, got very sad
When he lost the tail that he once had.
But he stopped being such a sad sack
When Robin found his tail and pinned it back.

There are few pleasures greater than sharing a book or story you loved as a child with a child you love. *Winnie the Pooh*, by A. A. Milne, has been a favorite in our family for four generations. We just couldn't resist writing a poem about it.

CHAPTER 7

A Child's Point of View

Young children are full of questions. A baby throws a spoon off of her high chair tray, then peers over the edge. Where did it go? You give it to her, and she immediately throws it down again. Will it make the same noise as before? Will you pick it up again?

Pointing is a favorite mode of question-asking for toddlers, sometimes accompanied with an all purpose word like *whazzat*? Two-year-olds learn to ask "What?" "Where?" and "Who?" Preschoolers also, and often incessantly, ask "Why?" and "How come?"

Children's questions are gifts. They let us know what children are thinking and what they make of the things we tell them. At the same time, they provide us with opportunities to clarify, elaborate, and explain. Good teachers and involved parents invite children's questions, making time to listen carefully and respond thoroughly.

A key way to prepare children to be successful and avid readers is to provide lots of experiences that will spark children's questions: new places to visit, interesting tools and musical instruments to try out, unusual textures or materials to experiment with, common and strange natural phenomena to investigate, construction sets and other toys that lend themselves to creative uses, or inviting books to read together. These experiences also give adults the opportunity to push children's thinking by asking *them* questions. Quizzing tends to shut down conversation. On the other hand, if you ask children many open-ended questions—questions whose answers you really want to know—you are likely to be surprised on a daily basis, both by the answers they give and by the understanding reflected in the new questions they ask.

Not all of children's questions, of course, have to do with gaining information. Just as we often ask children whether they have completed an assigned task or know a bit of information that we think it is important for them to learn, they often ask, "Why do I have to do that?" or "How come I can't?" Although sometimes their questions are simply attempts to delay doing something that they would rather not, a brief but genuine explanation will help them understand what is important and is likely to lead to more conversation.

This chapter addresses both kinds of questions. It includes playful and more serious poems about manners and good behavior and children's attempts to "do as they are told" or to evade compliance by only following the letter of the law. It also includes poems about the genuine questions children ask as they try to make sense of the things they hear and see in the world around them. Most of the poems in this chapter are written from a child's point of view, and all reflect the logic, misconceptions, curiosity, playfulness, and eagerness to please of children we have known.

We offer this collection for adults and children to enjoy together, in hopes that it will spark new questions and new learning opportunities.

Questions

I'm always asking questions.
There is so much I want to learn.
Why do we have elections?
And why do windmills turn?

Who goes up to polish the stars?
What kind of creatures are living on Mars?
Why won't my hair ever grow straight?
And why doesn't a verb reverberate?

Why does the candle keep dripping wax?
Why do you have to pay a tax?
Why does peeling onions make you cry?
Why is cotton candy hard to buy?

Why do you always want me to behave?
Why don't you like it when I rant and rave?
Why do the bumble bees swarm around trees,
And what is the matter with talking to bees?

Why do the light bulbs have to burn out?
And why can't a girl become a boy scout?
Why can't a camel ride an elevator?
And why can't I play with an alligator?

To a young child, the world is full of things that are new and things that don't quite make sense. What seems perfectly ordinary or logical to us inspires their wonder, consternation, or concern. When we stop to listen to their questions, we can seize these "teachable moments" to provide information, explanations, and reassurance that they will remember.

The more you share your knowledge, interests, and adult vocabulary with young children, the more questions they will ask and the more opportunities you will have to extend their learning.

Do Not Jump in the Puddles

It was a rainy, rainy day.
I wanted to go out and play.
"OK," said Mom.
"Put your raincoat on.
But do not *jump in the puddles.*"

I jumped on the sidewalk.
I jumped on the ground.
I jumped over the rope
And turned all around.
But I did not jump *in the puddles.*

I jumped in the sandbox.
I jumped on the rocks.
I took off my boots
And jumped in my socks.
But I did not jump *in the puddles.*

I put boats in the puddles.
I threw sand in the puddles.
And then I washed my hands
In the puddles.
But I did not *jump* in the puddles.

I walked in the puddles
I ran in the puddles.
I took off my coat and
I swam in the puddles.
But I did not *jump* in the puddles.

Now I'm as wet as I can be,
And there is mud all over me.
But I am proud. I was so good.
I did what Mommy said I should.
I did not *jump in the puddles.*

Young children are quite good at doing what we tell them to, avoiding things that we explicitly forbid, and getting into all kinds of creative trouble by doing something that we didn't even think of. The child in this poem manages to do exactly what her mother told her to and exactly what her mother was trying to prevent her from doing.

As you share the poem with children, see if they can pick up its humor. What did the child do? How did she feel about it? How do you think her mother felt when the child came home all wet? Do they think the poem is funny? What do they think might happen next?

The poem also highlights aspects of English grammar. Verses two and three focus on where the child jumped (everywhere but in the puddles). Verses four and five focus on what she did in the puddles (everything but jump). See if children can come up with new lines that tell where the child jumped or what she did in the puddles.

This is an easy poem for children to try to read on their own because so many words are repeated and the text is quite predictable (it's easy to guess what the next word or phrase might be, particularly if you have heard the poem before.) Beginning readers might like to make their own books illustrating the text or substituting some of their own lines. You can also write the poem on chart paper, using rebuses in place of (or in addition to) words like *raincoat, rope, sandbox, boots,* and *socks.* Children can then read the poem aloud together as you point to the words that they should say. Even the prereaders will enjoy shouting, "I did not jump in the puddles!"

Staying Healthy

I buy a lot of healthy food
When I go to the store.
But my Visa card was not renewed,
So I can't buy any more.

I wash my hands before I eat
(At least most of the time.)
But sometimes I am not so neat
Or can't get off the grime.

I use my toothbrush twice a day.
I get the toothpaste wet.
I brush each tooth just the right way—
Except when I forget.

I try to get a lot of sleep.
I even take a nap.
But I wake up when I hear a peep
Or even just a tap.

I use an umbrella when it rains
To keep my body dry.
I jump over the puddles and the drains.
Well—at least I try.

I do want to be healthy.
I know that health is good.
And so I try my best to do
All the things I should.

Healthy habits begin in early childhood, and children mainly learn them by copying the adults around them. It's also important for children to under-

continued

stand *why* these healthy habits are important. You can explain simply that healthy food—like milk, beans, fruit, vegetables, and whole grains—helps them grow strong and feel good. So does getting enough sleep and enough exercise. Washing their hands and brushing their teeth get rid of germs that can make them sick or cause cavities in their teeth. Dressing for the weather might not prevent them from getting sick, but it will make them more comfortable and make it easier for their bodies to fight off germs.

Every time you take a child to the supermarket, involve him in planning a menu or preparing a recipe, or read the labels on his cereal boxes or medications, you have opportunities to extend these lessons. As you talk together about what you are reading, the child will learn new words like *vitamin, carbohydrate,* and *protein,* and will also learn about how his body works and how to keep it healthy. He will understand that you are concerned for his welfare, and will see the value of literacy.

These lessons can be extended through pretend play. Give children a collection of healthy play foods: fruits, vegetables, milk, eggs, beans, and items that look as if they are made with whole grains. Also let them play with real packaging—cereal boxes, empty plastic bottles, and cans—that is not too heavy. You can also save food labels or cut pictures from grocery store advertisements and paste them onto paper bags or empty plastic containers.

Being Polite

I got this message from the birds:
Please and *thank you* are magic words.
If I want something I should ask, "Please."
I should say, "Excuse me" when I sneeze.

The birds also told me to be polite
And to wish you all sweet dreams at night.
And in the morning when I see the Sun
I should say, "Good morning" to everyone.

The birds told me that when I go to school
I should try to follow every rule.
When the teacher says sternly, "Don't give me that story"
I should tell the truth and say I am sorry.

I should keep on trying to be polite
And should always try to say things right.
And be sure to listen to the birds
When they chirp to me courteous words.

Manners can be difficult for young children, especially when they are in a hurry to get someone's attention or say something that just can't wait. At the same time, children love the idea of "magic words" and learn rather quickly that words like *please, thank you*, and *excuse me* have special power to command adult attention.

As you share this poem with children, take the opportunity to talk with them about the courteous or polite words they know and use. How do people react when they use these words? How do they react when people use these words with them? You might also talk together about what it really means to be polite. What are some things that people do that hurt others' feelings? How can polite words and actions make people feel better?

If children interact with people who speak other languages, teach them some polite words in those languages.

Birthday Party Manners

Take a dish of donuts.
Dunk them in your drink.
Dip them in your ice cream,
But do not turn them pink.

Take a dot of icing.
Dab it on your nose.
But do not drop it in your eyes
Or drip it on your clothes.

Dive into your presents.
Don't throw the cards away.
Please don't forget the thank yous
On your delightful day.

Although 1-year-olds are often encouraged to stick their fingers in their birthday cake and dunking donuts is a tradition at some fast food eateries, not everyone would see the instructions in this poem as good party manners. Placing a dab of icing on the birthday child's nose is a new tradition in some communities; diving into the presents is usual but not truly polite. "Thank yous," though, are a tradition that everyone can agree on.

Birthday parties are an easily recognizable part of American culture, and even toddlers often associate them with cake, ice cream, blowing out candles, and presents. Indeed, playing birthday party may be a favorite activity in the "house corner" or sandbox. A box of birthday party props (old cards, wrapping paper, tape, small toys, a tea set, used birthday candles, and perhaps some clay or play dough) can support this play routinely or be saved for a rainy day when a quick, fun activity is needed. Making birthday cards is also a great literacy activity.

This poem can also provide an opportunity to explore cultural differences. Are birthdays celebrated with parties in everyone's family? What do people do at the celebrations? What special foods are served?

For children learning letters and sounds, this poem is full of "delightful Ds." Can the children find them all?

Patience

"Patience is a virtue." My mother told me so.
And so I try my best to wait, but I really have to go.
I don't have too much patience, I really must confess.
When someone mentions waiting, I say, "No," not "Yes."

I'm always in a hurry. I have no time to kill.
When someone says, "Be patient," I just cannot sit still.
I get ants in my pants so I have to keep going.
Don't ask me why. I have no way of knowing.

"Patience is a virtue." I'm sure that it is true.
But I just have too many things that I just have to do.
And when I have to hurry and scurry all about,
Patience is a virtue that I can do without.

Waiting is a challenge for most young children, and words can help them cope. Knowing that the field trip will be "tomorrow," that daddy will pick them up "after lunch," and that they can go out to the playground "as soon as we finish cleaning up" helps children to feel in control, anticipate exciting events, and tolerate the wait. However, because young children don't have a good sense of time, their judgment about how long it takes for something to happen is determined by how much they like what they are doing rather than how much clock time has past. If a child is told that his friend will be over in 10 minutes, he might ask his mother every 2 minutes where his friend is. On the other hand, if he is told that he has only 10 more minutes to play before bedtime, he may protest vehemently when his mother tells him 15 minutes later that it's bedtime. "But, mommy, you promised me I still had 10 minutes to play."

As mother and daughter, we had to write this poem because neither of us quite managed to learn the patience our mothers tried to teach us—and neither did our children.

Being Reliable

I try to do the things I'm told.
I wear a sweater when it gets cold.
I eat my dinner when it's hot,
But I do not like to eat a lot.

Before I go in a room, I knock,
And I pay attention to the clock.
I listen for the clock to chime
And make sure that I am home on time.

You can always count on me.
I'll do things for you for free.
I'll put my clothes in the wash machine
And back in the drawer when they are clean.

I'm certain that if I am good
And do all of the things I know I should,
You will one day tell everyone
That you have a most reliable son.

Reliable is not a word that we would expect to use to describe any young child, but the lessons learned in early childhood do contribute to the development of this trait. When we teach toddlers to "touch gently," help them put toys away when they have finished, or show them how to turn pages without tearing them, we sow the seeds of reliability. When we provide children with regular routines and use words to help them know what will happen, we give them a sense of control. They are less likely to be upset by changes and transitions and are better able to anticipate special events. They also learn to think sequentially and to plan ahead. When we give children responsibilities that they can handle, such as taking care of library books or helping set the table, we strengthen their skills and boost their self-esteem.

Toddlers and preschoolers love to be helpful and show the important people in their lives that they too have important things to contribute and can be counted on for help.

Jasmine

Jasmine played with her toys all day,
But then she forgot to put them away.
Her dad said, "Put those toys on the shelf."
So Jasmine did it all by herself.

Jasmine's mother went away,
And Jasmine stayed at home to play.
She put some cocoa into a cup,
But then she forgot to drink it up.

Jasmine's father said to sweep the floor
While he and the baby went to the store.
Jasmine did what she was told,
But she left the door open and the house got cold.

Then Jasmine found something nice to do.
She put some polish on Dad's favorite shoe.
But before she could shine it, she started to feel
That it was time for her evening meal.

So she made a sandwich with peanut butter
And cut it in half with her mom's nail cutter.
But before she could finish her favorite meal,
She heard the sound of a tire squeal.

She went outside and saw the car
(Her family was back 'cause the store wasn't far.)
She helped her dad with a grocery sack
Then ran out saying, "I'll be back.

The car is all dirty. I'll get a pail
And give it a bath. I will not fail."
But before she could finish its wash and dry,
A whole lot of rain fell out of the sky.

continued

Poor Jasmine was feeling broken hearted
That she couldn't complete what she had started.
So she went to her room and took down her toys
And started to make a whole lot of noise.

Her mother came in, and guess what she said.
"It is time for you to go to bed.
But before you do, you should drink up
All of the cocoa you left in your cup."

"Don't you know, Mother, that I always do
All of the things that I start out to.
And, of course, you know I would never forget
The things that I haven't started yet."

Jasmine thinks of herself as reliable, and she really means to be. She tries to clean up after herself and do nice things for her family. It's just that her plans don't always work out. As you share this poem with children, see if they can follow the story. What things did Jasmine start and finish? What things did she forget? What could she finish tomorrow?

A wealth of interests and a desire to do things for themselves keep children like Jasmine constantly on the go. Before one project is finished, they are often on to another—eager to try new things and show everyone what they can do. You can help by setting aside space and time for long-term projects while helping children complete short-term tasks. For example, while children might be required to clean up before going outside, they might have a table or corner where they can keep their projects up for a week or more.

Long-term projects invite group play and problem solving, as children make decisions together about what to add to their growing constructions. Your involvement can extend the learning. There are all kinds of possibilities for literacy. A photographic record of the stages of the project, with captions that the children dictate, can help them tell and retell the story. Signs can provide explanations for visitors or warn them not to disturb the work in progress.

As children create a world together, they will tell stories that get more and more elaborate. Talking with adults about what they have built will reinforce pride in their work as well as their language and storytelling skills.

Why? Why? Why?

Why does the Sun go to bed at night?
Why did those children start a big fight?
Why won't my father let me play with a match?
And why aren't the chicken eggs starting to hatch?

Why does the north wind keep on blowing?
And why doesn't the hurricane know where he's going?
And why do I have to wear boots and a coat
When I splash in the puddles and watch the sticks float?

Why do I always have to wait?
Why is my school bus so often late?
And why is it 'cause of a traffic jam?
You can't put traffic on toast or eat it with ham!

Why don't some children like the circus parade?
Why do tigers in cages make them feel afraid?
Why do potatoes grow under the ground?
Why do you say that the world spins around?

For children with lots of questions, one answer is rarely enough. If you explain that the Sun doesn't really go down, the Earth just turns so that the Sun is hidden from our view, they'll want to know what makes the Earth turn and why they can't feel it spin. If you say that a traffic jam made the school bus late, they may want to know what caused the traffic jam, where all of the other cars were going, or why you use the same word to describe a long line of cars that they use for the stuff they like on their sandwiches. These persistent questioners can exasperate the most patient adult, but they are likely to become good students and lifelong learners.

One way to prepare for and encourage follow-up questions is to get a number of books on the same subject—both fiction and nonfiction. That way, when questions surpass your expertise or your patience, you can answer, "Let's see if this book will tell us." Meanwhile, you're teaching children valuable lessons: to persist in asking questions and in seeking answers through reading.

I Wonder

Do you ever ask the question,
As you squat upon a quilt,
And watch a line of ants come out
Of the city that they built—

How can creatures so, so small
Make a palace for their queen?
How can they build a city
Whose plans they've never seen?

They cannot use a T-square.
They cannot talk or hear.
Yet they built a perfect city.
Now don't you think that's queer?

The questions in this poem reflect a lot of prior knowledge as well as keen observation. As you share it with children, you may need to explain some of the terms and concepts. Have children seen an anthill? Is it home to one ant, a family, or a whole lot of ants? What do they think is inside? Do they know what a queen ant is? Does she really live in a palace? What do they know about building houses and cities? Have they ever seen a T-square or a blueprint?

You might organize children's prior knowledge and new questions by recording them on chart paper in two columns: "What We Know" and "What We Want to Know." The chart can guide further learning as you help children investigate anthills or an ant farm; record their observations in pictures, sculptures, or words; talk with classroom visitors who know about ants and other insects or about building plans, tools, and techniques; seek answers to their questions in books and on the Internet; and share their new knowledge with others.

For children who are learning their letters, this poem is also a good source of **Q** words. You might point out that, in English words, the letter **Q** is usually followed by the letter **U**. Do the children know anyone whose name starts with **Q**? Is the **Q** followed by a **U**?

I Want to Know

Why every morning does the Sun rise and shine?
Why is it yellow when the weather is fine?
And is it embarrassed at the end of the day
When its face gets all red and it hurries away?

When the clouds are all soft and puffy and white,
They look like the pillows I sleep on at night.
Who makes those cloud beds so high in the sky?
Are they cozy and warm and a nice place to lie?

And why are there sometimes no clouds at all?
When the sky turns all gray, do the cloud sleepers fall?
Do they hide in the trees and wait out the storm?
Do they shiver and freeze till the weather gets warm?

Why does the thunder roll loudly away?
Where does it roll to and why won't it stay?
Why does rain fill up puddles and run down the street?
And how come a snowman never has feet?

Why does a hurricane have only one eye?
Does the wind get in it and make it cry?
When they say a storm is coming, how do they know?
Who tells those strong winds that it's time to blow?

As you share this poem with children, engage them in conversation about some of its questions and imagery. What do they think a roll of thunder sounds like? Does it sound more like a drum roll, or more like a heavy ball rolling across the floor? How would they make a thunder noise? What do the clouds look like to them? What do they think a cloud would feel like if they could touch one?

The questions in this poem reflect misconceptions that are common among children. Some come from observation and analogy, others from knowing only some of the meanings of common words like *roll* and *eye*. The answers to questions like these may be difficult for young ones to grasp. At the same time, their own explanations are charming and also reveal active, logical minds that are busy putting together information from different sources. How can you satisfy their curiosity without squelching their wonder, creativity, and emergent reasoning?

There isn't one right way to handle children's difficult questions, but rather a number of approaches that teachers and parents have found helpful. Which ones you use will depend on the ages and interest levels of the children.

- Ask children what they think. Can they say it in words? Can they draw a picture?

- Help children to be good observers. For example, they might keep a weather log or draw pictures of the sky at different times. They can put out a cup or rain gauge to collect and measure rain, watch a puddle and draw its picture for several days in a row, or draw sunset pictures and then compare the colors they used with the colors they see during a week of sunsets.

- Encourage children to make predictions and then see if what they expected to happen did.

- Provide a simple explanation that will satisfy them for the moment, even if it is not the whole story. For example, you might say that lightning is electricity that moves through the sky very, very fast, and it makes the air explode. Find opportunities to introduce more sophisticated explanations through books and conversation as children show more interest.

- Provide experiences that will help children understand. For example, you can show them the "cloud" that rises from a teakettle or the condensation that collects on a cold glass.

- Admit when you don't know, and search for answers together.

Too Many Questions

You're always asking questions!
You always bother me.
How on earth should I know
Why whales swim in the sea?

Why do you think that I might know
What spots are on the Sun?
Or why that lady wears her hair
In that ridiculous bun?

Please tell me the reason that
You ask me all the time
Why a word like *seventeen*
Doesn't have a rhyme?

Why must you always ask me
Why the sky is painted blue?
You know I would not tell you
Even if I knew.

How often must I tell you
That I really do not know
Why turtles slip inside their shells
And what makes turnips grow.

Why do you keep on asking me
Why the world is round?
You know I can't see far away
When I am on the ground.

You know I cannot tell you,
So why do you keep asking
Why masking tape holds pictures up
But is not used for masking?

continued

You ask so many questions.
It really is an art.
I guess I'll have to answer you,
So we can both get smart.

As you share this poem with children, remind them that asking questions is an important way to learn. Grown-ups might not be able to answer all of their questions right away, but they still want them to keep asking "so we can all get smart."

To encourage children to keep asking questions, some parents like to add "question time" to their bedtime ritual or substitute it for reading time on occasion. Some teachers like to keep a question box near the writing corner or a questions folder on the computer. When children think of a question that can't be answered right away, they can dictate it to a teacher. Questions can be pulled out of the box or folder for group discussion and investigation at regularly scheduled times or whenever an unexpected event interferes with your plans and you need a quick substitute activity. Other teachers post children's most interesting questions on a bulletin board or put them in their portfolios. That way, parents can appreciate their children's intelligence and curiosity and also seize opportunities to pursue emerging interests.

Perseverance

Henry was trying to fix Santa's sleigh.
His mother said, "Why don't you throw it away?
It cannot be fixed. There is no chance at all.
So why don't you go outside and play ball?"

Henry answered her with a sigh,
"I know you are right but I still want to try.
I almost had it fixed before,
So I think I will try just a little bit more."

Henry kept trying and trying all day,
And just before dinner, he'd mended the sleigh.
"I was sure it was something that I could do,
And now it looks even better than new."

"Tomorrow," he said, "I will build a new shelf.
I'm sure I can do it all by myself."
He hammered and nailed and put in a screw,
And the shelf was all finished by quarter of two.

Next Henry decided to clean up the lawn.
It had been neglected for ever so long.
By the time he got finished it looked pretty good.
His dad said, "You're like the Little Engine that Could."

Few children have Henry's talents, but all can master challenges with appropriate support. As you help children complete the tasks they set for themselves, resist the urge to solve their problems and fix their mistakes. Instead, use observations and questions to call their attention to successes and problems, to encourage their predictions and inferences, and to help them figure out what to try next. Indeed, when we take children's ambitions seriously and give them the time, space, and support to complete tasks to their own satisfaction, we teach them the rewards of perseverance.

CHAPTER
8

Colors, Shapes, Numbers, and Opposites

Learning to read depends on understanding the meanings of words, how words go together to form sentences, and how sentences go together to tell stories or convey information. It involves knowledge of how words are represented in print and, for a language that is written with an alphabet, how letters and letter combinations represent the sounds that make up words. It also involves tuning in to patterns.

Poems highlight sound patterns that are critical for reading; with repetition, the recognition of these patterns becomes automatic. Skilled readers automatically divide words into syllables, recognize common letter combinations and meaningful word endings, and use their knowledge of sound patterns, word structure, grammar, and logic to anticipate words as they read. Beginners use these cues to catch their mistakes or to help them figure out a new or difficult word.

Knowledge of colors, shapes, numbers, and opposites is not essential for reading, but it can play an important role. Children who have learned

129

to sort, classify, talk about likes and differences, and count can tune in to patterns that are based on these concepts. The concepts provide tools for quickly organizing experience; playing with them provides practice in using this organization to predict what is coming next or recognize when something doesn't fit.

Children who can recognize colors and shapes, who have a good understanding of number, and who can match common opposite pairs will understand color, shape, number, and direction words when they encounter them in reading. They will be able to guess the meaning of a new word when the context makes it clear that its meaning is the opposite of one that they know (e.g., Next to her tiny baby, the mother kangaroo looked *gigantic*). Their experience with patterns of all sorts will have primed them to notice patterns in print and in stories, and their recognition of these patterns will enhance both their reading fluency and their enjoyment of what they are reading.

Colors, shapes, numbers, and opposites also play key roles in many of the problems that we ask young children to solve, as well as in problems that they set for themselves. Whether a child is ordering the rings on a ring stacker, nesting a group of containers, retrieving a ball that got stuck behind a couch, assembling a puzzle, following a recipe, negotiating an obstacle course, putting together a multipiece toy, building a bridge for toy cars, or simply setting the table, language can play an important role. The more practice children get in using language to solve problems, the more adept they will be—both at solving problems and at using precise, descriptive language. You can help by doing the following:

- Thinking aloud: We need three more napkins, one for Jae Lin, one for Kirstie, and one for Marisol.

- Asking questions: Which one do you think comes next?

- Helping children correct mistakes: Oops. The yellow one was too big. Can you find one that is just a little bit smaller?

- Using quantitative terms with children: We need 4 ounces of water, 1 cup of flour, and 1 teaspoon of salt.

- Using words that describe direction and location: It's on the third shelf, between the yellow book and the green one.

- Encouraging children to make comparisons: Which end is heavier?

- Encouraging children to make and test predictions: Do you think the pencil will be long enough to reach the ball, or do we need to get the baseball bat?

- Challenging children to follow multistep directions: First put two wheels on each axle and then snap the axles onto the frame.

- Helping children to make logical connections and draw logical conclusions: Animals are living things that move, breathe, and eat. Is a tree an animal? Are you an animal?

By the time they get to kindergarten, most children know a lot about colors, shapes, numbers, opposites, and patterns—even if they can't "name all their colors" or recognize every numeral. To support, enhance, and celebrate their growing knowledge, we offer this collection of playful, patterned poems.

Colors

Green is the color of grass and of trees.
Green is the color of a plateful of peas.
Green is the color of a light that means go.
It could be the color of a house that you know.

Yellow is the color of a daisy's eye
And of mustard and corn and banana cream pie.
Yellow is the color of the sun when it's bright
And the soft, mellow color of candlelight.

White is the color of clouds, snow, and ice,
Of seashells and sea gulls and little white mice.
White is the color of a Halloween ghost
Or a peeled potato you're about to roast.

Red is the color you see when you're mad.
Red Riding Hood tells us that red is not bad.
Red is a fire engine whizzing by fast
And a sign that says STOP before you go past.

Blue is the color of the clear daylight sky.
It's the color of berries you put in your pie.
Blue is how you feel when you don't want to smile.
Blue is a moon you see once in awhile.

Brown is the color of tree trunks and wood.
Brown is the color of things that taste good—
Like syrup, molasses, and very dark honeys
And baked beans and peanuts and chocolate bunnies.

Black is the color you see in the night.
Black is your room when you turn off the light.
Black is the color of a very deep hole.
Black is the color of burnt toast and coal.

continued

Orange is the color of carrots to munch
And oranges and peaches to eat with your lunch.
Orange is the color of a crossing guard's vest.
I think it's the color that I like the best.

This poem can get children started thinking about the colors of things that they see around them. What colors are their favorite foods? Can they name some foods that are their favorite colors? What colors are the people around them wearing? Do they see any colors that are not mentioned in the poem?

Some of the verses refer to metaphorical meanings of color words. You may have to explain "seeing red," "once in a blue moon," and "feeling blue" if children have not heard these phrases.

Learning colors is especially fun when children can make them up themselves. Given paints or dyes of different colors, children often mix them all together and end up with brown, which may or may not be the color they wanted. However, you can set up the activity in a way that encourages experimentation and conversation.

- Give each of three or four children a different color of tempera paint. What colors can each pair of children make by putting their paints together? What happens when the whole group combines colors? What happens when you use a little of one color and a lot of another?

- Fill a long, shallow container with water. Have children help put several drops of food coloring at one end and several drops of a different color at the other. Then add several drops of liquid soap and watch the colors mix.

- Make homemade play dough with the children, using different food coloring colors. Let the children mix different colors of play dough to see what new colors they can make.

- Make a paint set in an egg carton by filling each cup with a mixture of half water and half school glue. Help children add a few drops of food coloring to each cup, in different combinations, until they get colors they like. Using cotton swabs as paintbrushes, let children use their custom colors to paint on wood or rocks or to make collages.

My Favorite Color

Brown is the color of mudpies and dirt
That you should try not to get on your shirt.
It is also the color of telephone poles
And hamsters and chipmunks, field mice and moles.

Brown is the color of brownies you eat.
Brown is the color of the shoes on my feet.
Brown is the color of some people's hair
And some people's eyes and the clothes that they wear.

You can make brown paint out of orange and blue.
You can make it from purple and yellow paint, too.
Brown is a color I'm happy to see.
It's my favorite color—the color of ME!

This poem celebrates the color brown: the color of many children's skin, hair, or eyes. Children can enjoy finding many things in their kitchen, classroom, or yard that exhibit different shades of brown. They might even like to make a brown collection and learn (or invent) names like *beige, tan, coffee,* or *pinecone* for the many shades of brown that they see around them.

Children may also get interested in "the colors of me." You can get crayons and paints in a range of skin and hair colors or mix the colors yourselves. Encourage children to find colors that match their own skin and hair. Create a class portrait by having each child color a stick or hand puppet or a paper cutout. You can also trace children's bodies on large brown paper, sketch in the clothes, and let children work together to paint themselves. Respect the children's color choices—they are unlikely to be able to find exact matches and may make different selections than you would. Encourage children to talk about the choices they have made and about all of the beautiful colors that people come in.

Shape Walk

I wanted to go for a walk.
It was a sunny day.
I started out to leave my house.
A rectangle blocked my way.

I reached out with my little hand
And turned a circle round.
It opened up the door and then
I stepped out on the ground.

I started to go down the street
But had to stop, you see,
When I came upon an octagon
That said S-T-O-P.

On I went and on some more
Past a house with a triangle top.
I walked till I got to my favorite park
And then I decided to stop.

On the ground I saw a diamond.
On each corner was a square.
Then someone swung a long, long stick,
And a sphere flew through the air.

When I got home from my shape walk,
I had a lot to say
About all of the shapely things
I came across today.

As you read the poem with children, point out the names and pictures of each shape. Can the children identify the object that is being described? Would the children like to go on a shape walk, either around the room or outside? They might look for a particular shape, see what different shapes they can find, or play I Spy and see if others can guess what they are looking at as they give shape clues. *Colors, Shapes, Numbers, and Opposites* • **135**

What Can You Do With a Ring?

What can you do with a ring, a ring?
What can you do with a ring?
A ring is just a round, roll-y thing,
So what can you do with a ring?

A ring is the ding
Of the bell by the door
Or the ring ring-a-ling
Of the phone on the floor.

A ring is for wearing
On fingers or toes.
You can even wear rings
In your ears or your nose.

A ring is where circus clowns
Show off their tricks
And make people smile
With their hoops and their sticks.

Rings are for juggling
And throwing up high.
You can hold onto rings
And make yourself fly.

A ring that's for swimming in
Keeps you afloat.
A ring can be blown
By the smoke of a boat.

A ring is a thing that you
Make with your friends.
When you all form a line
That doesn't have ends.

continued

Now sing *Ring Around the Rosy*
With daises in your hair.
Or dip a ring in bubbles
And make rainbows everywhere.

There are rings under our glasses
And around our napkins, too.
Our baby has rings to chew on
When her teeth are very new.

I have rings in my cereal bowl
And rings in my game.
My new puppy Snoopy
Has two rings in her name.

Oh there's lots to do with a ring, a ring.
There's lots do with a ring.
A ring is just a round, roll-y thing,
But there's lots to do with a ring.

This poem works on two levels. On the one hand, it is about a simple shape—a ring or a circle—that is found in a variety of places. You might challenge children to find all of the rings that they can see from where they are sitting or to think of other places where rings can be found.

The poem also introduces the idea that one word can have multiple meanings. Most of the "rings" in the poem are things that are circular in shape. Children might like to draw pictures of some of these rings or to make one picture with lots of rings in it. Other rings, however, are sounds. Can children identify these?

If children get interested in words with multiple meanings, you might follow up by finding (or making) a book of riddles.

Who Knows One?

Who knows one?
I know one.
One is my nose
That sneezes and blows.

Who knows two?
I know two.
Two are my eyes
That widen with surprise.

Who knows three?
I know three.
Three wheels on my trike
Take me anywhere I like.

Who knows four?
I know four.
Four legs on a chair
At the corners of a square.

Who knows five?
I know five.
Five points on a star
You can see from afar.

Who knows six?
I know six.
Six legs on a bug
That crawls across the rug.

Who knows seven?
I know seven.
Seven days, counting Monday
Going all the way to Sunday.

continued

Who knows eight?
I know eight.
Eight sides on a sign
That says, "STOP behind this line."

Who knows nine?
I know nine.
Nine Chanukah lights
On a menorah shining bright.

Who knows ten?
I know ten.
Ten toes on my feet
For dancing in the street.
'Cause I know ten!

As you share this poem with children, enlist their help in responding to its questions. What can they think of to illustrate each number? A group of children might like to say the poem in chorus, with one person asking the questions and others responding. On *ten*, they can all stand up and dance.

Children who like the poem might like to make their own number books. Help them put each numeral on a separate page. They can then draw a picture that illustrates that numeral (like a hand with five fingers), or they can stamp a simple shape the correct number of times, counting as they go.

Here are some other ways to help children "know" numbers.

- Give children a die to play with. They will soon learn to "see" the numbers without counting. When they can recognize the numbers on one die, encourage them to play with two. What numbers can they make? How many ways can they make a number like seven?

- Put five small objects, such as beans, in your hand. Ask a child to take some and hide them in his fist. Then tell him how many are in his hand. Two-year-olds may think it's "magic" that you can count objects without seeing them. After awhile, however, they will realize that when they can see four, one is missing; when they can see three, two are missing; and so forth.

Birthday Woes

"I'm sad," complained Samantha,
When she was turning four.
"Jake is three. Now we can't be
The same age any more."

"Don't fret," said her mother.
"I will end your sorrow.
Let's bake a cake for your friend Jake.
His birthday is tomorrow."

"Then he'll be four," Samantha asked,
"And I will be four, too?"
"Yes, that's right. Tomorrow night
Jake will be four like you."

Many young children make Samantha's mistake. Even if they understand that their age is the number of years since their birth (unless they come from a culture where age is figured from before birth), they have no way of counting those years. To them, the number of fingers you hold up when someone asks how old you are has magic significance, and four is significantly older than three.

The poem, of course, only begins to provide an explanation. You may want to show children their birthdays on a calendar and talk about how long it will be until they get to their next age. Be sure to give them concrete markers: in the winter, after your sister's birthday, right before Thanksgiving, when you go to kindergarten, and so forth.

Countdown

Rocket, rocket are you ready
To shoot up in the air?
I will start the countdown now
So you can prepare.

Ten, nine,
Eight, seven, six.
Is there anything
To fix?

Five, four,
Three, two, one.
Now the countdown
Is all done.

Zero. Blast off!
Fly up high
As your fire
Lights the sky.

Once children get good at counting forward, they can learn to count backward. If they like this countdown, encourage them to help you say the counting backward lines. They may decide to incorporate countdowns into their space launch pretend play. Being able to count backward quickly will come in handy when they learn to subtract.

Finger plays, like *One Little Garbage Truck* (see Chapter 6, page 107), give children practice counting forward and backward and associating one finger with each number. Although some teachers discourage it, counting on your fingers is actually a very good way to solve addition and subtraction problems. Most children have to start at one and count out each of the numbers that they are trying to add, and fingers are useful for keeping track. For example, to add 3 + 2, they would count "one, two, three," then "four, five." It takes a long time before children can "count on" by starting at three and simply counting "four, five."

How Much Is a Million?

The dinosaur bones at the science museum
Are 65 million years old.
I see a million stars at night.
At least, that's what I'm told.

I can build myself a castle
From a million grains of sand.
But how much is a million?
I don't quite understand.

I have 5 fingers on each hand.
Together that makes 10.
If I add in all 10 wiggly toes,
I get to 20, then.

There are 5 of us in my family.
If I count all of our fingers and toes,
It adds up to 100.
That much I do know.

If I put 100 jelly beans
Inside an empty jar,
Then lined up 10 full jars like that,
I'd get pretty far.

I'd have 1,000 jelly beans
Sitting on my shelf.
One thousand yummy jelly beans—
Too much to eat myself.

I could take 10 jars of jelly beans
And pack them in a crate.
If I had 10 crates of jelly beans,
That really would be great!

continued

I'd have 10,000 jelly beans.
I could open up a store.
Do you think there'd be enough to feed
A hungry dinosaur?

I could open 100 jelly bean stores
All across the land.
If I had a million jelly beans.
Yes, now I understand.

Many young children are fascinated by big things and big numbers—the bigger the better. For budding mathematicians, this poem presents some sophisticated concepts. It helps them learn the powers of ten that will be key to understanding place value and scientific notation, and also helps give them a sense of how much is a million. These concepts will be beyond most young children, but preschoolers will be able to grasp the idea that a hundred is bigger than ten, a thousand is bigger than a hundred, and a million is bigger than a thousand. They might like to fill jars with jelly beans (or plain beans), try to guess how many they can hold, and then work together to figure out how close they came. Encourage them to count by making groups of ten and then counting by tens.

Counting By

Two, four, six, eight—
I think trucks are really great.
Three, six, nine, twelve—
Twelve tiny trucks up on the shelf.

Five, ten, fifteen, twenty—
Now I think that we have plenty.
If you feel that we need more
You will have to keep the score.

Counting by twos, threes, or fives helps children count more efficiently.
Counting by groups of numbers is a precursor to multiplication. As with
one-to-one counting, children can learn the sequence by rote as they are
learning the concept. With the counting-by patterns firmly in their heads,
learning the multiplication tables becomes a much easier task.

This short poem will get children started in counting by twos, threes,
and fives. Encourage children to play out this poem with real objects, such
as miniature trucks or animals, as well as to memorize the lines.

Opposites

Big is the opposite of small.
Short is the opposite of tall.
Good is the opposite of bad,
And happy is the opposite of sad.

Day is the opposite of night.
Dark is the opposite of light.
Whisper is the opposite of shout,
And in is the opposite of out.

Dirty is the opposite of clean.
Nice is the opposite of mean.
Empty is the opposite of full,
And push is the opposite of pull.

Fat is the opposite of thin.
End is the opposite of begin.
Take is the opposite of give,
And die is the opposite of live.

And More Opposites

Some things go up and some things go down.
Some people smile and some people frown.
Some things are white and some things are black.
I live in the front and you live in the back.

Some things are hot and some things are cold.
Some things are new and some things are old.
Some cars go fast and some cars go slow.
Some lights mean stop and some lights mean go.

Some diamonds are real and some diamonds are fake.
Sometimes I give and sometimes I take.
Some shelves are high and some shelves are low.
Sometimes I say, "Yes" and sometimes I say, "No."

Some things are expensive and some are cheap.
Some lakes are shallow and some are deep.
Sometimes I'm early; sometimes I'm late.
Some foods I love and some foods I hate.

These poems introduce children to the idea of opposites. After sharing the
poems with them, you might want to play some opposite games. Start with
the poems themselves. If you read the beginning of a line, can children fill in
the last word? Can they do it without the additional cue of a rhyme? (In this
case, make sure they know that there can be more than one right answer. For
example, *whisper* could be the opposite of *scream* or *yell* as well as *shout*.
Nice could be the opposite of *nasty, ugly,* or *bad* as well as *mean*.) If children
enjoy the game, encourage them to quiz you and also to play with their
friends. Can they think of other opposite pairs that are not in the poems?

Ruby Gets a Cat

Ruby this and Ruby that
Ruby sees a yellow cat.
Ruby then and Ruby now
The cat sees Ruby and says, "Meow."

Ruby one and Ruby two
"Look, Cat. See what I can do!"
Ruby three and Ruby four
"Look out, Cat. Here comes some more!

Ruby five and Ruby six
Cat likes all of Ruby's tricks!
Ruby seven, Ruby eight
Cat jumps up on school yard gate.

Ruby nine and Ruby ten
Ruby gets her down again.
Ruby messy, Ruby neat
Cat rubs up on Ruby's feet.

Ruby yes and Ruby no
Ruby says, "I've got to go."
Ruby don't and Ruby do
Ruby runs and Cat runs too.

Ruby rich and Ruby poor
Cat meets Ruby at the door.
Ruby slip and Ruby slide
"OK. Cat. Come on inside."

Ruby down and Ruby up
Ruby finds an old brown cup.
Ruby satin, Ruby silk
Ruby gives the cat some milk.

continued

Ruby go and Ruby stop
Cat laps the milk up—every drop.
Ruby frown and Ruby smile
"I wish that you could stay awhile."

Ruby happy, Ruby sad
"Hide, Cat. Quick! Here comes my dad."
Ruby hard and Ruby soft
Dad yells, "Scat!" and Cat takes off.

Ruby thank you, Ruby please
Ruby gets down on her knees.
Ruby ask and Ruby beg
Cat rubs up on Daddy's leg.

Ruby him and Ruby her
Cat looks up and starts to purr.
Ruby jumper, Ruby leaper
Dad says, "OK. We can keep her."

Ruby Gets a Cat was inspired by a jump rope rhyme. Like many such rhymes, it includes frequently paired words. Can children identify words that are opposites, as well as pairs of words that are similar in meaning? Can they follow or retell the story of how Ruby got her cat?

As you share the poem repeatedly with children, you might encourage them to clap out the rhythm, clapping loudest on the last word of each line. They might enjoy saying these words with you or filling in the words themselves while you simply clap.

Like jump rope and hand-clapping rhymes, *Ruby Gets a Cat* lends itself to choral reading. Children who are learning to read might enjoy reading it together if you post the words on a chart or give each child a copy. Children who are not yet reading might enjoy learning one or two verses to say in a group or chiming in while others read.

This poem was coauthored by reading specialist Linda Rath.

CHAPTER
9

Going Places

Pretend play is the hallmark of early childhood. It creates and sustains friendships, promotes intellectual growth, and encourages language development. Pretend play enables children to cope with bad or sad feelings and to feel good about themselves. It is also one of the most effective and delightful ways to foster emergent literacy.

As children engage in role-play, they may act out a series of events in a logical sequence. For example, they might write out a shopping list, go to the supermarket, pay for their purchases with play money, return home, and put the groceries away. They may plan an exciting adventure, pack up their gear, trudge around the playground, chase away wild animals, jump across a river, or discover hidden treasure—returning home triumphant. In the course of these activities, children challenge themselves to create rich narratives with more and more complex story scripts. The stories that they play out often reflect their understanding of the underlying structure of stories that they have been read or told about real or imaginary events.

Pretend play can also familiarize children with printed words. As they play grocery store, for example, children may look at labels on packages and numbers on play money and cash register keys. They may incorporate pretend writing as they play out a restaurant scene in which the patrons are given menus with pretend writing, the waiter writes down the order by scratching random squiggles on a pad, and the waitress presents a bill at the end of the meal. The children are motivated to "write" because writing serves a real purpose for the grown-ups they are imitating.

Reading and writing can also serve a real purpose for the children themselves. Children who are putting on a show may ask the teacher to help them write the program, create a billboard, or make signs that they can hold up at the appropriate times during the performance such as GOLDILOCKS AND THE THREE BEARS, APPLAUSE, INTERMISSION, and THE END. Children who are playing pirates may want to make a treasure map or secret code.

When adults get involved, pretend play can be an even more powerful impetus to language, literacy, and social–emotional development. Adults can set the stage for pretending by arranging the environment; by providing inspiration through trips, books, stories, and other activities; and by supplying props and costumes. They can help children create costumes, scenery, doll clothes, and attractive play environments such as forts and playhouses. They can add print in various forms to enhance these environments: an appointment book and prescription pad for the veterinarian's office, brochures and tickets for the travel agency, or blueprints and warning signs for the construction site.

Adults can enhance ongoing play by supplying requested information, making suggestions, and introducing new ideas and vocabulary as they talk with children about what they are doing. They can add new elements or suggest new directions if the play becomes repetitive, too wild, or unsatisfying. Of course, if a child is being hurt, ignored, excluded, or taken advantage of, adults need to intervene. Helping children talk through such problems and use their creativity to find a better role for the victimized child usually results in both happier children and more satisfying play. These techniques provide opportunities for children to learn and use more sophisticated language as they listen to each other, propose solutions, negotiate, and think through problems together. Thinking about how storybook characters solve problems similar to theirs can often help children make their own play more fun for everyone.

Adults can encourage the extension of play by providing opportunities for children to create an ongoing story in an environment such as a dollhouse, playhouse, or block corner that can stay the way the children left it; by encouraging children to turn their play into a puppet show or staged play; or by helping children make books that tell stories that they first created in their pretend play.

By far the most powerful way that adults can support children's pretending, and its power to enhance literacy, is to join in the fun. An adult who takes on a role—as a restaurant customer, demanding baby, circus performer, or even just appreciative audience—has all sorts of opportunities to challenge children's thinking, extend their stories, introduce new words and ideas, and accompany them on new adventures.

For great pretenders and their adult playmates, we offer this collection of poems to begin your imaginary journeys.

Books

Every time I read a book,
I want to read one more.
On every single page I look,
I find something I adore.

I read about places far away
Where I would love to go.
I try to read a book each day
There's so much I want to know.

I read a book the other day
About lizards, toads, and frogs
And creatures that live far away
On mountains and on logs.

Every single book I read
Sparks my imagination
And lets me go at break neck speed
On my next vacation.

The books I read I always keep
Very near my light.
And just before I fall sleep,
I kiss my books good night.

Like the child in the poem, many of us have experienced the joy of being lost in a book and transported to another realm. The books we love touch our hearts, engage our minds, and fuel our imaginations. They provide us with beautiful language and imagery, characters who become our friends, and thrilling plots that compel our interest. They also provide us with topics for conversation and reflection. For us, literacy isn't just about being able to read, it's also about love for the written and spoken word and the ability to appreciate and learn from the messages they contain.

Children who enjoy being read to are often motivated to "read" themselves. As they pretend to read to themselves or to a doll, they have an opportunity to demonstrate and practice book-handling skills. These skills include turning the pages from left to right, holding the book so that the "audience" can see what you are reading, or pointing to an illustration or a word that you expect your audience to look at. Placing dolls or stuffed animals in the reading corner is one way to facilitate this behavior.

As children pretend to read books whose words they have memorized, they sometimes slide over into real reading as they associate words on the page with words that they are saying.

Going to Town

Would you like to hear about my town?
There is a lot to tell you, so I've written it down.
We have a beautiful city hall
And a gigantic shopping mall.

There is a city park where I love to go
And a theater with a picture show.
And if you just walk down the street,
There are so many people you'll want to meet.

There is a supermarket where you can buy
Anything that catches your eye.
They have shopping carts that you can ride.
You'll have lots of fun when we go inside.

There is a pizza place just down the street
That serves lots of stuff I like to eat.
You can get a salad with anchovies
Or a fresh, hot pizza with extra cheese.

There is also a library where we could go.
They let us check out books, you know.
The last time we went there, I checked out three.
So why don't you go in there with me?

The town described in this poem could be a real place, but it could also be a
play town built from blocks, miniature toys, or child-sized furniture and
cardboard boxes. Here are some fun ways to make a play town into what
experts call a "literacy-rich environment."

- Incorporate print into scenery, as appropriate. For example, you might have a sign for a store or restaurant, a mailbox and a welcome mat at the entrance to a home, a sign that says Tickets on a ticket booth, or an Emergency sign at the hospital or animal hospital.

- Include props that contain real print: empty food packages in the grocery store or kitchen; postcards, maps, and travel brochures for the airport or travel agency; train schedules, newspapers, subway maps, and tickets for commuters; or numbered jerseys, team caps, programs, score cards, and autographed items for ballplayers.

- Solicit parents' help in collecting labels from products that their children use at home, especially those that reflect their and cultures and the languages spoken in their homes.

- Use print on costumes, hats, nametags, and badges.

- Provide appropriate writing materials and props such as ledgers, envelopes, checkbooks, prescription pads, order blanks, chalkboards, and trip logs.

- Encourage children to make their own props, such as menus, placemats, play money, treasure maps, tickets, invitations, valentines, crowns, flags, banners, street signs, and sports insignia, using art and writing materials or a computer.

- Supply children with street signs, labeled buildings, and labeled vehicles to use in building cities, towns, farms, and imaginary worlds.

- Provide inspiration through books and posters showing real cities, farms, bridges, and buildings.

- Furnish measuring and planning tools such as tape measures, rulers, and graph paper for drawing plans and maps, blueprints, and schematic drawings.

- Take pictures of children's constructions for their portfolios or scrapbooks or to post as inspiration for others.

- Take before, during, and after pictures of a project and let children put them in order and dictate captions.

- Provide signs that children can use to temporarily protect their constructions.

Going to a Restaurant

I went to a restaurant with my mother.
I brought along a book.
I tried to show it to my brother,
But he refused to look.

So I took my box of crayons
And said, "Wouldn't it be neat,
If you drew a pretty picture
Of the things you'd like to eat?"

He drew a great big pizza
And colored in each slice
While I ordered from the menu.
"Rigatoni would be nice."

I ate my rigatoni
With lots of extra cheese.
That platter made me fatter,
But I always like to please.

My brother ate his pizza
And politely wiped his lip.
We thanked the waitress for our food
And gave her a nice tip.

We paid the cashier for our food,
And then we went outside.
We were too full for walking,
So we took a taxi ride.

A trip to a real restaurant can be a wonderful opportunity to expand young
children's vocabularies, their ability to use language, their knowledge of the
world, and their emergent literacy. You might talk with them about the

continued

items on the menu: what they taste like, how they are cooked, where they come from, or what sounds appealing and what doesn't. Encourage children to order politely and to ask questions if they are not sure what they would like. They might create their own illustrated menus while waiting for their food, or you can talk about all of the steps involved in food preparation.

You might also take the opportunity to do some math together: "How many tables do you think there are in the restaurant?" "How many people do they feed each day?" "How many pizzas can they fit in their oven?"

Pretend restaurant play can be even richer, especially when an adult takes on the role of a demanding customer with unusual tastes. "Oh, thank you for my peppermint stick ice cream cone. It's delicious. But do you have any sprinkles? Chocolate or rainbow? Which do you recommend? Do you have any hazelnuts? I always like nuts on my ice cream cones, and hazelnuts are my favorite. Oh, this cone is getting drippy. Do you have a sundae cup I could put it in? I think I'll put some butterscotch sauce on it and maybe some anchovies."

A more elaborate approach is to help children create their own pretend restaurant complete with a name and logo, placemats, menus, order blanks, wait staff, and chefs. Adults can support the planning and provide whatever help is needed in gathering and creating materials. Then the children can get the restaurant ready for its grand opening. After enjoying their meals, the adults can show their appreciation with a hefty "tip" or a rave review for the local "newspaper."

The sillier you are, and the more elements you toss in when you play your part, the more creative children will be as they play with each other—and the more chances they will have to extend and practice new skills.

Supermarkets

Supermarkets are a good place to shop
When you get to the market come to a stop.
And then you must hurry to go inside
So that you can go on a basket ride.
Start by taking out your grocery list
Make sure that there's nothing that you have missed.

If you need peanut butter or apple pie
Take it off the shelf if it isn't too high.
Then go to the aisle where they keep all the candy
A chocolate bar may come in handy.
Don't forget to buy some chicken or fish
And take out bottled water if you wish.

Fill your basket to the top
That is what you do when you shop.
When you're ready to leave the store go to the cashier
And tell her you're happy that you came here.

Trips to the grocery store can be great opportunities to promote emergent literacy. At the same time, literacy-building activities can turn a potentially stressful chore into a fun adventure. You might start with having children help you make a grocery list. A 2-year-old might notice that you are running out of her favorite cereal and be able to help you glue the box top onto your "list"; a 3-year-old might be able to draw a picture or squiggle that she can "read" to indicate what she wants to buy; a 4-year-old may be able to write some of the letters.

At the store, you can read children the sign for each aisle and help them figure out which items on their list might be found there. You can also take the opportunity to talk with them about the items you buy and the ones you reject. Show children how you check prices and food labels. Talk about why certain foods are healthy; how to tell if produce is ripe or fresh; and the

continued

colors, tastes, and textures of different foods. Talk together about the foods you need for breakfast, lunch, dinner, and snacks. Try to find something that each person in the family or class likes. With older children, you can talk about where foods are grown or how they are used in the cuisines of different cultures. Send children after particular cereals or soups or ingredients for a special meal. As they shop, children will be learning new words; putting items into categories; learning about nutrition, cooking, and culture; thinking about others' needs as well as their own; planning ahead; recognizing logos and letters; and tuning into the multiple uses of reading, writing, and math.

When children play store, the possibilities for learning are similar. You might work with a group of children to set up a play supermarket. Talk together about types of props that they will need. Explain how to use empty boxes and play money. Make price labels to help support their literacy. Talk about organizing the store into categories—fruits, vegetables, frozen food— and making signs for the aisles. Create specialty aisles (or a specialty market like a bodega or deli) to reflect the children's heritage or a culture that they have been learning about. (Be sure to include packaging and signs in the appropriate language, even if you can't read or understand the words.) Encourage children to take on roles as customers, cashiers, and shelf stockers as they play in their store together. Once in awhile, when you go into the store to shop, ask for their help in finding things on your list: both items that are available and those like "alligator food" or "seaweed cake" that might not be.

Under My Umbrella

I put up my umbrella
If the sun gets much too hot.
I use it when it's raining
And also when it's not!

Under my umbrella
Is where I like to be.
When the sun is shining brightly
And the sand is under me.

"At the beach" is a great pretend game to play with children, especially on a rainy day. You can lay out a few towels, grab an umbrella, pack up a real or pretend picnic basket, and throw in some seashells or beach toys. A storybook or illustrated shore guide can inspire the pretending or supply new ideas if needed.

Some families and teachers like to create theme boxes, or collections of key props, that relate to the children's interests and experiences or to their favorite books. They bring out a theme box when the children show a particular interest or seem to need new play ideas; when interest wanes, they put it away for another day. Common theme boxes include the following:

- Beach: shells, pebbles, starfish, shovel, pail, towel, picnic basket and play food, and empty sunscreen container.

- Doctor/veterinarian: doctor's kit, bandages, prescription pads, and pencil.

- Restaurant: menus, order forms, paper placemats that children can decorate, and packaging from fast food restaurants.

- Train ride: whistle, engineer's cap, tickets, and hole punch.

- Travel agency: tickets, travel brochures, souvenirs, post cards, and maps.

As you put together theme boxes, think about how you can include print materials such as catalogs and packaging along with props that inspire pretend reading and writing.

At the Corner Candy Store

At the corner candy store
The counter's always full
Of lollipops and lemon drops
And taffy you can pull.

There are multicolored candy canes
And long, long licorice laces.
You'll always see a crowd of kids
With smiles across their faces.

Carmella likes the caramels.
Carlitos takes the cake.
Colin counts out candy corn
To share with Uncle Jake.

Gus goes for the gummy bears.
Willie wants the worms.
At the corner candy store
It's hard to wait your turn.

After you share this verse with your class, put out some candy store props
for dramatic play. These could include a Corner Candy Store sign, OPEN
and CLOSED signs, paper bags, a cash register, money, baskets, boxes,
string, ribbons, a telephone, and an assortment of pretend candies made out
of paper or clay. Join the children as they decide who should be in the store.
You can suggest customers, sales persons, a manager, and a baker.

Expand the children's vocabulary by talking about all of the ingredients
needed to make candy. Ask the children to pretend that they are making candy.

For children who are learning letters, this poem and the candy store it
describes are great sources of **C** words. You might focus on words with a /k/
(hard c) sound, as in corner and candy, before talking about the /ch/ and /s/
sounds in words like chewy, licorice, and ceiling. Do they know any people
with **C**s in their names? Do the **C**s sound like Kim, Siloene, or Charles?

Playing Ball

I am pretty good at basketball,
But I'd be a lot better if I were tall.
Then I could jump high and dunk a few,
And the ball would go where I asked it to.

I thought that baseball would be my best sport,
Because you know I'm a little bit short.
But every time the pitcher throws balls at me,
The ump shouts, "You're out. That's strike three."

Then I decided I would try out tennis.
When I serve the ball I am truly a menace.
But sometimes the ball goes into the net,
And a zero score is all that I get.

Well, you know, they say there is no use crying.
All you can do is keep trying and trying.
There's soccer and football and volleyball.
Someday, maybe, I'll be good at them all!

When I am grown up very tall,
I will be able to play basketball.
I might lose sometimes, but mostly I'll win,
Because I'll make the ball go in.

Many young children share a love of sports with their parents or older siblings. Over time, they learn the rules of the game and are able to follow the play. Once they understand the basics, a game becomes like a story: it has heroes or heroines, plot twists, and often a dramatic climax. In their fantasy play, these children may cast themselves as the heroes who make the winning goal or the game-saving catch.

There are lots of ways to capitalize on children's interest in sports in order to build their literacy skill. As you talk with them about how a game is played or the triumphs and errors of their favorite players, you can introduce specific vocabulary. You can play a sport together with an imaginary ball and help them learn to create more complex scenarios. You can set up a score board together for a real or imaginary game; point out the names and numbers of their favorite players; help them learn to recognize team logos; and put logos, letters, and numbers on costumes that they wear while they pretend to be sports heroes.

For many children, the daily sports page will be among the first things they read on their own. You can feed their interest by reading sports books together, even as you share other types of books that you particularly enjoy. For most children, sports are one interest among many. For some, though, they are the connection to a beloved family member and also a gateway to reading and math.

Gabe's Goofy Goggles

Gabe got goofy goggles
For swimming in the pool.
One day he brought his goggles
To share with us at school.

Gail tried on the goggles.
She said, "Now I can fly.
Watch me be a pilot
Going high up in the sky."

Gaston put on the goggles
And said, "Hey, can you hear
How my motorcycle engine
Roars when it's in gear?"

Goldie took the goggles.
She said, "Everyone watch me.
I'm going after grouper fish
At the bottom of the sea."

Garrett wore the goggles.
He said, "These are really cool!
Now I can be a jeweler,
Grinding a tiny jewel."

When Gabe got back his goggles,
He said, "You guys are first rate.
Without your help I couldn't have known
My goggles were so great!"

Like puppets, large cardboard boxes, and wagons, goggles are a great toy
because they suggest many uses but don't constrain the play. Children are

continued

especially delighted with the idea of "magic" goggles. When they put on a pair of these goggles, they can do anything they want to do, be anyone they want to be, or go anywhere they want to go. When they wear their goggles they can see every room in the house, any country in the world, or any star in the universe. When they wear their magic goggles they are afraid of nothing. Children are not a bit scared of the dragon that sleeps under their bed, and they just bark back when the ferocious dog that lives next door starts barking at them. They never worry about what to do next. Wearing their goggles, children can go to a circus, visit their very best cousin, or fly to the moon in a spaceship.

Imaginary goggles, made by putting your fingers around your eyes, can help interest children in a new experience or help them make a transition. "Put on your goggles," a teacher says to the children. "We are about to zoom out to the playground in a speedy motor boat. Look carefully. We might see some dolphins." When it is time for dismissal, the teacher asks the children to put on the goggles again. "Put your goggles on as fast as you can. Your family is about to land in a helicopter and fly you to the rainforest."

If you can collect some old swim goggles, eyeglass frames, or cheap sunglasses, you might put a basket of "goggles" in a dramatic play area.

For children who are learning their letters, *Gabe's Goofy Goggles* is replete with Gs. You might ask the children to go on a treasure hunt to see how many gs they can find in this poem. Talk about how most of the Gs make a /g/ sound (hard G), as in goofy, but the G in engine sounds like the J in jewel. Ask the children if they know anyone with Gs in their names. Also ask them what sounds these Gs make.

Going Exploring

I went outside the other day.
I decided it was time to go away.
I thought I should go to the equator,
But I was afraid of an alligator.

So I decided it was best
To take a walk to the far west.
When I got to the Pacific sea,
I was stung by a bumblebee.

I planned then to go back east.
I did not want to encounter a beast.
I walked around for a day or so
When suddenly it started to snow.

I really wasn't cold at all,
So I made a very big snowball.
I was about to throw my ball away,
When some nice children asked me to play.

We played all day and built a fort
Surrounded by a huge seaport.
When we discovered we had cold feet,
We went to my friends' place to eat.

I ate as much as I was able,
And then had to leave the table.
I thanked my friends and waved goodbye,
And then I looked up at the sky.

Outside of their house it was very dark,
And a scary dog began to bark.
I decided then I should not roam,
So I hurried back to my warm home.

continued

My mother kissed me right away,
And asked me if I had a fine day.
I told her that the day was kind of boring,
So I went to bed and started snoring.

Young children make up stories like this every day. Unconstrained by the real world, they wander from adventure to adventure. They cross continents and oceans, escape from scary beasts, make new friends, build forts, make snowballs—all in a day's play.

The stories that children act out as they play alone or with friends also make great books. When children have been particularly creative in their pretend play, ask them if they'd like to be authors. If they are interested, ask them to tell you about what they played as you write down their words. Try to start each incident or adventure on a new page.

Read the story back to the children, and ask them to make some pictures to go with it. Then encourage them to "edit" the books: putting pictures where they belong, making sure that the pages are in order, and adding anything they forgot. Put the finished books in the library or reading corner and encourage the children to "read" them to you, themselves, and each other.

Can You Help Me Fix My Wagon?

My wagon's wheel is wobbly.
It's not exactly tight.
Will you help me fix it?
Can you help me make it right?

I wonder why it wobbles
And what we need to do.
Can we fix it with a hammer?
Does it need an extra screw?

When we have fixed my wagon,
We both can sit inside.
It will be so exciting
To take a wagon ride.

As you share this poem with children, take on the role of the child who needs help. Interrupt your reading to solicit their ideas on what you can do: "Are there other ways that you can think of to fix my wagon?" "What do you think might be wrong?" "Could you bring it to a bike shop and ask the manager to fix it?" "Could you go to a gas station and fill its tires with air?"

When you encounter real things that need fixing, be sure to involve the children in the problem solving. Encourage them to ask questions, make hypotheses as to what is wrong or what could work, and help find the appropriate tools to use to try out their best ideas.

For children who enjoy being letter detectives, this poem is filled with Ws and Xs. How many of each can they find?

North Pole

If you want to go to the North Pole,
I can tell you how.
Get inside a blanket roll,
And drive in a snowplow.

When you see a reindeer,
Ask it where you are.
Tell the deer why you are here
Right under the North Star.

Take a big sledgehammer—
Pound a stick into a hole.
Put up a giant sized banner
Saying, "I Got to the North Pole."

The North Pole has been a popular fantasy destination for generations of young children. Some have thought of it as a sort of flagpole that is stuck on top of the world; others have thought of it as Santa's home. A few may understand that it has something to do with where a compass needle points. As you share the poem with children, you might talk with them about their ideas of what and where the North Pole is, whether anyone lives there, and how they might go about getting there if they wanted to.

Of course, a pretend expedition to the North Pole can be lots of fun, and it can keep a group busy for quite awhile. First, they'll need to see where they are going on a map or globe, and they may want to make their own maps to plan the route. The children will have to decide whether to go by land, sea, or air—perhaps going by all of these. Second, they'll need tickets for the journey. Third, a packing list will be critical. The children will need to make sure that they have compasses and binoculars, along with appropriate clothing, tents, food, communications equipment, and other gear. Finally, of course, they'll need that "giant sized banner" to prove that they were there. A collection of North Pole books—both nonfiction and fiction—can further enhance these literacy-building opportunities.

Annabelle the Astronaut

Annabelle, the astronaut, zoomed into space.
She stayed many days in a very tight place.
Then she docked her rocket at a space station—
Her favorite place to take a vacation.

She had lots of adventures as she floated up
there,
High above planet Earth, past the clouds and the
air.
She put on her space suit and went out each day,
Tied to a tether so she wouldn't float away.

She gazed at some galaxies studded with stars
And took lots of pictures of Venus and of Mars.
And when it was time to blast off again,
Annabelle counted backward from ten.

This poem, like much of children's pretending, mixes real information with fantasy. As you share Annabelle's adventure with children, first help them understand the words. Do they know what an astronaut is? Can a girl or a woman be an astronaut? Do they know what the poet means by "she stayed many days in a very tight place?" (The space shuttle is the size of a large jet. Its journey to the International Space Station takes 3 days. The earlier spacecraft that carried the first astronauts into orbit and that took the first men to the moon were much smaller. Some children may have seen these capsules in museums or may have seen pictures of them in books.)

As you share this poem with children, talk about the words *astronaut, planet, tether, galaxy, blast off, Venus,* and *Mars*. Find books that illustrate these terms and that can help you explain their meanings. You might also want to show children the NASA Web site (www.nasa.gov), where they can see images from space flights and telescopes and learn even more interesting facts and vocabulary.

Celebrations

Would you like to go to a celebration
Where there are flags from every nation?
It would be a nice thing to do.
And if you ask me, I'll take you.

We could go to a coronation
Of a queen in the highest station.
And when the queen puts on her crown,
The bells will ring all over town.

We could go to a parade
That features a fire brigade.
And when the marching bands pass by,
We will hold our flag up high.

Celebrations of all sorts are great fun for children, who enjoy the opportunity to participate in a special event with adults and older children.

The period leading up to the celebration provides numerous opportunities for adults and children to participate together in literacy activities: checking newspaper or poster announcements for public events, sending out invitations to private celebrations, making shopping and to do lists, getting or giving directions, reading related storybooks, preparing special recipes, making menus or place cards for guests, learning special songs, making signs and decorations, marking off days until the event on a calendar, and lots of talking about the exciting things that are going to happen.

The celebration itself is likely to provide a new set of language and literacy-building opportunities: new people to meet; special costumes, banners, and rituals to talk about; new foods to taste and describe; new experiences that evoke new questions; memories of past celebrations to share and compare; and chances to perform and sing along. Afterward, there will be many chances to remember the experience in conversations, photo albums, and reenactment, as well as to begin to plan for next year.

Feeling Fine

When we're together in good weather,
It makes me feel so spry.
I could throw a feather in the heather
Just to watch it fly.

Do you know where we could go
To see a country fair?
With giant slides and pony rides
And lots of food to share?

We'll eat fried dough and cones of snow
And ride the carousel.
We'll toss some rings and pull some strings
And ding the winners' bell.

Some cotton candy would be dandy,
While we hear happy tunes.
We'll find your mother and my brother
And buy them both balloons.

This poem has a rollicking rhythm that matches its light-hearted words. Children might enjoy saying the first verse together, as they hold hands and sway to the beat or skip out to the playground.

The poem also introduces some new vocabulary: *spry, heather, country fair, carousel, snow cone, cotton candy,* and *fried dough.* Children might enjoy learning what heather looks like and how it grows and what fried dough, snow cones, and cotton candy taste like. They might enjoy other songs and rhymes about fairs such as the nursery rhyme *Simple Simon.*

Such poems might get children started on a multicultural exploration of fairs and festivals. You might use chart paper and help children make lists of things that one can see, hear, taste, and smell at different festivals or fairs. The children may even want to create a fair of their own. Making invitations, price tags, and signs for booths will give them lots of literacy practice.

Story Poems

Storytelling is an ancient art and the basis of literature. It began as a communal event, with an audience gathered around to hear an account of a recent adventure or a sacred story that was handed down from generation to generation. Traditional storytellers often encouraged the audience to participate by asking questions, repeating familiar refrains, and urging the storyteller on with words of agreement or challenge.

Traditional stories from around the world share many common elements. Like most stories that get retold or written down, they have a beginning, a middle, and an end. The beginning sets the stage, the middle contains a problem to be a solved or an obstacle (or series of obstacles) to be overcome, and the ending includes a resolution of the problem. The stories often follow a distinct pattern, for example, facing three challenges or succeeding on the third try. The pattern may be marked by a repeated refrain that gives the audience an opportunity to chime in or prepares them to be surprised by a twist at the end. Often the stories come full circle, ending in the place they began, with everyone having learned something.

Traditional stories, whether oral or written, are likely to use poetic or literary language. This language has many special features:

- It often uses literary devices, such as alliteration and rhyme that call attention to the sounds of words.

- It is likely to be more descriptive than spoken language, containing more adjectives and adverbs.

- It may contain rare words that expand children's vocabularies or spark questions.

- Its sentences are likely to be longer and more complex than those of "ordinary" language.

- Whether or not it rhymes, it may have a special rhythm and cadence.

Exposure to literary language and traditional story forms provides important preparation for reading. It gives children practice in hearing and understanding the kind of language they will encounter in print. It teaches them to follow a story, making connections between related events. It stretches their vocabularies. And, of course, it instills a love for the spoken and written word and for a "good story."

What makes a story special to a young child, however, is not only what it contains, but also what the people who share it with him bring to the reading, telling, and retelling. Speaking in different voices, exaggerating sound effects, making a game of naming pictures or chanting the chorus together, repeating funny words and tongue twisters, reminiscing about shared adventures, letting the child tell parts of the story, and drawing parallels to the child's own experience are just a few of the techniques that you can use.

For storytellers and their participating audiences, we offer this collection of old tales retold and original story poems.

Fuzzy Bear

Fuzzy Bear woke up one day
And hurried to go out to play.
He looked both ways and crossed the street
And tried to find some friends to meet.

He decided to go down to the lake
To see if his lake friends were awake.
He found a friend and they started to play.
They had a wonderful time all day.

Then Fuzzy felt a grumble in his tummy.
"Its time to go home and get something yummy."
He didn't want his mom and dad to worry,
So he raced for home in a very big hurry.

On his way home he came to a tree,
And in the tree there was a bee.
Perhaps he could ask the bee for honey,
But he did not have any money.

"Please" and "Thank you" he said to the bee,
Who was busy buzzing in the tree.
But Fuzzy didn't say another word.
Talking to bees was quite absurd.

Next he came to a city park.
He realized it was getting dark.
Fuzzy Bear didn't stop to play.
He hurried on along his way.

Now he knew just where to go.
At least he thought that he should know.
He thought that he would get home soon,
If he followed the light of the moon.

continued

He knew that it was time for bed,
So he kept on walking straight ahead.
But then he heard a terrible sound.
It was the bark of an angry hound.

"Help! Help!" called Fuzzy. "I don't know
If it's north or south that I should go."
Poor Fuzzy Bear began to weep,
And pretty soon he fell asleep.

He dreamed he was home in his nice warm bed—
Under the covers and very well fed.
"Could it be true?" he thought when he heard a sound,
"Could his mother dad be somewhere around?"

He opened his eyes up very wide.
His mother and dad were by his side.
"Oh, Honey," they said to Fuzzy Bear.
"We could not find you anywhere."

"We looked and looked all over the place,
And we could not find your sweet little face.
Now promise us that you will not stray.
Home is the very best place to stay."

"Let's hurry home so you can eat.
We saved you some honey for a treat.
If you were gone, what would we do?
We could never find another you."

Fuzzy ate all his dinner and went upstairs.
His parents helped him say his prayers.
And after his favorite story was read,
They gave him six kisses and tucked him in bed.

continued

Fuzzy Bear follows a pattern that will be familiar to young children who have heard many stories. It starts in the morning and ends at night. It begins with getting up and ends with going to bed. Its main character strays too far from home and stays away too long, eventually getting lost. After some scary experiences, he is found and brought home by loving parents.

It is no accident that a lot of stories for young children are like *Fuzzy Bear*. Young children use parents and other familiar people as a base of support. Following their natural curiosity, they stray farther and farther from this base as they gain confidence in their ability to explore their world and find their way "back home." Although a real young child would never stay out alone all day, a storybook character can act out every child's fear of being lost or abandoned. Hearing the story gives him the chance to reaffirm that he, too, is deeply loved and will always be brought safely home.

As you share the story with children, pause between its sections to talk with them about how Fuzzy Bear is feeling and what might happen next. Be sure to give each child who wants them a hug and "six kisses" when you finish. Encourage a child to play out Fuzzy's story by speaking for Fuzzy as you go out for a walk, play, try to come home, and get lost. Let the child be the parent who finds you and brings you home.

The Three Little Pigs

Once upon a time there were three little pigs—
Two sisters and a brother.
And all of them lived in a wee little house
With their father and their mother.

When the three little pigs were mostly grown,
They wanted houses that would be their own.
"Goodbye," said Mom. "Goodbye," said Dad.
"Watch out for the wolf cause he is BAD."

The first pig built a house with hay.
She worked on it for one whole day.
She made the walls; she made the floor.
The wolf came knocking on the door.

"Little pig, little pig, let me come in."
"Not by the hair of my chinny-chin-chin!"
"Then I'll huff and I'll puff and I'll blow your house in!"

He huffed with a smile; he huffed with a frown,
And the little hay house came tumbling down.
The little pig said, "What can I do?"
And she ran to find pig number two.

The two little pigs worked all day long
To build a stick house big and strong.
They made the walls; they made the floor.
The wolf came knocking on the door.

"Little pigs, little pigs, let me come in."
"Not by the hair of our chinny-chin-chins!"
"Then I'll huff and I'll puff and I'll blow your house in!"

continued

He huffed with a smile; he huffed with a frown,
But the strong stick house did not fall down.
Then he huffed so hard that his face turned blue.
The stick house fell and away it flew.

The little pigs said, "This cannot be!"
And they ran to find pig number three.
The third little pig had a load of bricks—
Stronger than hay and stronger than sticks.

The three little pigs worked all day long
To build their brick house big and strong.
They made the walls; they made the floor.
The wolf came knocking on the door.

"Little pigs, little pigs, let me come in."
"Not by the hair of our chinny-chin-chins!"
"Then I'll huff and I'll puff and I'll blow your house in!"

He huffed with a smile, he huffed with a frown,
But the strong brick house did not fall down.
Then he huffed so hard that his face turned blue,
And his tail and his whiskers turned blue, too.

He puffed so hard that his fur turned brown,
But still the house did not fall down.
He puffed so hard that the sky turned black,
And he blew away and he never came back.

The three little pigs danced all night long
In their own brick house that was big and strong.
And they lived happily ever after.

continued

The Three Little Pigs is a classic children's tale from England. In the original tale, the first two pigs get eaten by the wolf after he blows down their houses, and the wolf gets boiled after being tricked by the third little pig. Children have enjoyed—and been frightened by—variants of the tale for generations. Some parents and teachers feel that the original tale is too violent for young children. Others are concerned that the tale sends a subtle message that people who live in European-style brick houses are somehow smarter than people whose homes are made of wood or straw. Our version remains true to the original in that there are three pigs, three houses, and three chances to say, "Then I'll huff and I'll puff and I'll blow your house in!" It differs, however, in that all of the pigs build the brick house together, cooperation wins the day, and no one gets eaten.

As you share this story with children, include them in the fun. Encourage them to chime in or take over the refrains: "Not by the hair of our chinny-chin-chins!" and "Then I'll huff and I'll puff and I'll blow your house in." Let them take on the part of the wolf and blow as hard as they can.

Also encourage children to talk about the story. You might ask a few short answer questions: "What did the first little pig use to build his house?" "Do you think the little pigs are scared of the wolf?" You can also ask some open-ended questions: "How do you think the little pig felt when the wolf blew his house down?" "What do you think he is going to do now?" Help children connect the story to their own experiences: "Have you ever seen hay?" "How could you build a house with it?" "Have you ever seen anyone building with bricks? Can you tell about it?" "Do you think bricks are really stronger than wood or hay? Why?"

The Three Little Pigs lends itself to retelling and reenactment. Children might like to replay the story with blocks and miniature animals, work together to make a mural or picture book, or put on a play or puppet show. Or they might pick up just one element from the story to incorporate into their play. For example, children might decide that the best way to clean up the block corner is to "blow" their houses down before putting away the blocks. They might protect their construction that they wanted to save with signs saying "No wolves allowed" or "Do not blow down."

If children know other versions of the story, talk with them about the similarities and differences. "Which versions do they prefer?" "What do they like about them?" Some children might like to make their own books, combining elements they like from different versions, or, in good folktale tradition, making up elements of their own. They can start by drawing pictures and then dictate the captions to you.

The Distinctly Extinct Dinosaur

I never, ever saw one before,
But today I saw a dinosaur.
Dad said, "You're being silly, son.
You must have seen a picture of one."

"No, Dad, He was really, real,
And he had lots of sex appeal."
Dad said, "I know that you like to pretend,
But a dinosaur is not a good friend."

I knew my dad could not be right.
A dinosaur would never fight.
And the dinosaur I saw today
Didn't want to fight. He wanted to play.

I went outside so I could see
If the dinosaur would talk to me.
Something I noticed was a surprise.
He wore glasses on his eyes.

He looked down at me and then he said,
"I think I would like to go to bed."
I asked him if he was feeling well
And if he was staying in a hotel.

"Oh, no," he said, "That is not what I'll do.
I am making plans to go home with you."
I couldn't think of anything to say.
I was hoping he would get out of my way.

"I'll go home with you," he said with a smile,
"But I'll only stay for a little while.
I just want to meet your mom and dad
If you won't let me I'll get very mad."

continued

I did not want the dinosaur
To get very mad or even sore.
"Okay, Dinosaur, have it your way.
Come to my house. It's a good place to stay."

I brought the dinosaur home with me
I wanted Mom and Dad to see
That no matter what some people think,
Dinosaurs are not extinct.

After dinner I found a book.
I just wanted to take a look.
I wanted to learn a little bit more
About the extinction of the dinosaur.

The book said, "Dinosaurs *are* extinct."
But that is not correct, I think.
At least one dinosaur lives on our street.
Come over tonight and you two can meet.

I know Dinosaur doesn't want to intrude,
And I am certain he would never be rude.
I invited him for dinner tonight.
I am sure that my parents will say it's all right.

He stayed for dinner and slept on our roof,
And now I feel I have substantive proof.
That dinosaurs still exist today,
No matter what anyone has to say.

And the next thing I plan to do
Is to call in a media crew.
And when you watch the news tonight,
You'll find out that I am perfectly right.

continued

The Distinctly Extinct Dinosaur follows a time-honored tradition by pitting the factual adult world against the magical realm that imaginative young children inhabit. As you read this story to children, help them follow the story by using different voices for the different characters. Use a high voice for the child narrator, and try to sound earnest and convincing. Use a low, serious voice for the father. Give the dinosaur a deep and unusual voice, perhaps using the ponderous tones of a record (or CD) played at slow speed.

Young children who know a lot about dinosaurs are likely to get much of the story's humor. They will realize that the dinosaur is just pretend, even though the boy keeps saying that he is real. They will know that dinosaurs did not wear glasses, that they are extinct (which means that we can't see them today), and that many were too big to fit through the door of a house or hotel or sleep on a bed. (Most children probably won't know that some dinosaurs were as small as chickens, even when full grown.) Other children may need to be clued in.

Similarly, you might check to see whether children understand terms like *sex appeal, intrude, substantive proof,* and *media crew.* You might also talk with children about the difference between stories in books and on TV that are meant to be true and stories that are meant to be just pretend.

The Knee High Man

There once was a man who came up to your knee.
He went for a walk to see what he could see.
He came to a field filled with grass and clover
And a big high fence that he couldn't see over.

So Knee High Man said to a mooing cow,
"I want to get big. Can you tell me how?"
The cow said, "Now, here's what you do.
Eat lots of grass and chew, chew, chew."

So Knee High Man, he tried that trick,
But the grass gave him gas and got him sick.
The chew, chew, chewing just made him start mooing.
He said, "This is NOT what I should be doing."

Then Knee High Man asked a horse, "What should I do
If I want to grow as big as you?"
The horse, of course, said, "Eat lots of hay,
And think big thoughts seven times a day."

So Knee High Man, he tried that trick,
But the hay made him neigh and got him sick.
The big thoughts he was thinking just hurt his head.
"Guess I'll have to try something else," he said.

So Knee High Man asked Owl, who was very wise,
"How can I get to be a bigger size?"
"It doesn't matter," said Owl, "what size you are.
What counts, my friend, is how wise you are."

"You think you'll see more if you are tall,
But there's a lot to see that's very small.
So get down on the ground and look around.
There is so much wonder to be found."

continued

Knee High Man got down and what did he see?
A snail with a tail by a mushroom tree.
A butterfly on a buttercup flower
And a frog in a fountain taking a shower.

Then Owl said, "Man, if you still want to see
What's over the fence, just climb my tree."
Knee High Man climbed up and what did he see?
What did he see from the top of that tree?

Just another field full of grass and clover
And another high fence that he couldn't see over.
"Thank you, Owl," he said, climbing down the tree,
"You taught me my size is just right for me."

The Knee High Man is an African-American folktale with special resonance
for young children. Its main character is a very small man who wants very
much to be "a bigger size."

As you share the poem with children, play up its humor. Use different
voices for the different animal characters. You can also use exaggerated gestures and facial expressions to emphasize the animals' advice and the results
of Knee High Man's attempts to follow it. Encourage children to join you
and to take on roles as they get familiar with the poem or can predict what
will happen.

You might also talk with children about the message of the story. Why
might a small person want to be big? Are there things that small people can
do that are harder for big people?

The poem might also inspire children to "get down on the ground and
look around" to find out what they can see "that's very small." Children
might look under rocks or old leaves, in crevices, near puddles or streams,
and inside of flowers to see what interesting things they can find. A magni-
fying glass can enhance the experience.

Another way to give children experience with different perspectives is
to give them simple cameras or even just paper towel rolls or pieces of cardboard with different shaped cutouts. Encourage children to describe what
they see as they look through these devices. Do they pick out details that
they didn't notice when they could see the whole scene?

Song of the Long Haul Trucks

The trucks yawn in the cool of the morning,
Thumbing their noses at patches of ice.
The trucks chitter-chat as they bump along dirt roads,
Then fill up for gas as they ask for advice.

The trucks purr as they roll along steady,
Humming their tunes when there's no one to hear.
The trucks smile when their friends come to join them,
Calling out greetings to small fry and peers.

The trucks sing on the long, open highways.
With nothing to stop them, they speed along free.
The trucks whisper in the snows of the mountains,
Then snake down the slopes as they yodel with glee.

The trucks grump in the traffic-full city.
They whine and complain as they wait for the lights.
The trucks moan through detours and back streets,
Inching through crowds that aren't always polite.

The trucks scream when they have to stop suddenly.
The trucks groan when the hills are too steep.
The trucks roar as they race to the finish.
The trucks sigh when they finally can sleep.

Song of the Long Haul Trucks follows the familiar story pattern of wake up in the morning, set out on an excursion, return home, and go to sleep. It is unusual, though, in that its main characters are trucks that are given human feelings and voices. The vocabulary is deliberately challenging so that children will get more out of repeated readings.

You might begin by reading the whole poem aloud, without interruption, so that children can enjoy the sounds. On repeated readings, you can

continued

talk about where the trucks are going and what they might be carrying. You can also talk about how the truck drivers feel at different points in the journey and how the sounds the trucks make might reflect the drivers' feelings. As you read, you can encourage children to make the appropriate sounds.

As children become more familiar with the poem, you can pause in your reading to talk about words or metaphors that they might not fully understand. Can a truck yawn? What does a yawn sound like? What does a truck sound like when you start it on a cold morning? What are "small fry" and "peers"? What vehicles would be "small fry" or "peers" for a big truck? Do they know what a "slope" or a "detour" is? Can they guess what these words might mean from how they are used in the poem?

Children who like trucks might like to act out this poem in the block corner, perhaps creating their own versions of hills, country and city roads, and garages. They might also like to make maps of a truck's journey and to investigate what real trucks look like and the different kinds of loads that they are designed to carry.

Tidalik

There once was a frog
Who lived in a bog.
His name was Tidalik.
He got in a muddle
And drank up a puddle,
Which made him kind of sick.

So he tried to get cool
By drinking a pool,
But that didn't work too well.
He drank up a pond
And the ocean beyond,
Which made his body swell.

All the animals around
Made a very sad sound,
'Cause they could not swim or drink.
Their eyes got so dry
They had no tears to cry,
So they all sat down to think.

Then an old kangaroo
Said, "I know what to do!
We will make him laugh out loud!
Then he'll sputter and spout
Making water gush out."
"What a great idea," said the crowd.

Koala stood on his head
Till his face got red,
And his friends all laughed with glee.
But Tidalik stood
Like a block of wood.
He didn't even say, "Hee-hee."

continued

The next to try
Was a black magpie,
Who sang a ridiculous song.
The kookaburra bird
Looked quite absurd,
As she danced and pranced along.

But Tidalik just sat
Looking big and fat,
And round as a red rubber ball.
He sat all night
With his mouth shut tight,
And he barely moved at all.

When morning came
And it did not rain,
The animals were thirsty and hot.
They panted and tumbled
And ranted and rumbled,
But did Tidalik laugh? He did not!

Then a lowly worm
Began to squirm
And crawled up on Tidalik's chin.
She wiggled and wiggled
Until Tidalik giggled,
And his mouth spread way out in a grin!

His dribble and drool
Filled the puddle and pool,
As he smiled and sputtered and jiggled.
It filled up the pond and the ocean beyond,
As Tidalik giggled and giggled.

continued

Everyone joined him
For a happy swim.
They splashed and dashed and floated.
Tidalik felt good
Looking like he should,
'Cause he was no longer bloated.

Now when Tidalik drinks,
He stops and thinks.
And he takes no more than his share.
He laughs and plays
Through all his days,
And his friends are glad he's there.

The tale of *Tidalik* comes to us from Australia, an island continent with many animals that live nowhere else in the world. One of these animals is the Crucifix Frog, which got its name from the cross on its back. The Crucifix Frog lives in dry places and spends most of its life underground. When it rains, these frogs come up to the surface, fill up with water, and then go back underground.

Today, there are many versions of the *Tidalik* story. The original story is part of a series of traditional tales that Aboriginal peoples (the original inhabitants) in Australia tell about the Dreamtime, the time before people came into the world.

As you share the poem with children, encourage them to take on the roles of the various animals that try to make Tidalik laugh. Can they act out each animal's antics? What other tricks would they try?

You might also use the poem to introduce an exploration of Australia's unique animals and cultures or discuss where water goes after it rains. These explorations can help children to appreciate the importance of conserving water and discover ways to save water in their daily lives.

CHAPTER
11

Help Me Learn My ABCs

To read independently, children need to know a lot about words, books, stories, and the world around them. Most of reading is comprehension—understanding and appreciating what one is reading. But this is dependent on the ability to rapidly and automatically recognize the words. Fluent readers look very briefly at each letter, but their brains process the familiar letters and letter combinations so rapidly that most of the time they are only aware of the words.

To get to the point at which they can read unfamiliar text fluently, beginning readers need to learn to "break the code." Children who can name some letters, recognize words that rhyme or that begin with the same sound, and blend word parts together (*d-og = dog*) can understand the "alphabetic principle"—the idea that letters and letter combinations represent the sounds that make up words. Later, they can learn to recognize common letter combinations like *-on*, *-ing*, and *-eat* and to sound out regularly spelled words by applying their knowledge of letters and their associated sounds and their understanding of how these sounds are likely to combine.

Knowing the names of the letters helps children understand reading and writing instruction. It also helps them to figure out the sounds that the letters represent, as most letters stand for sounds that are similar to their names. Writing is important because it helps children to make the link between the written and spoken word and to tune in to the way in which words are constructed. As they see the words they say represented on paper, children make the critical link between the spoken word and its representation in writing. As they try to communicate with the marks they make and then write "real letters," children often work out the alphabetic principle for themselves.

Children are introduced to letters in many ways. They may wear a T-shirt with words on it, watch their teacher point to the words as she reads a story, or see their own name written on the picture that they drew at school. They pretend to write by drawing a squiggly line or by drawing letterlike shapes that only they can "read." They learn to recognize oft-seen symbols: a big **M** means McDonalds, the buttons in an elevator tell it what floor to go to, and a big red sign means stop. They may read *ABC* books, play with alphabet blocks, and learn to sing the *ABC* song. Young children are likely to recognize the first letter in their name and may assume that anything that has their letter on it belongs to them. These early discoveries prepare children to learn alphabet concepts.

Learning the names of the letters and their sounds used to be a central task of the kindergarten or first grade curriculum, but today children are expected to recognize at least ten letters before they get to school. They may also be expected to know some letter sounds and be able to identify objects whose names begin with commonly used consonants such as *b, d, g, l, m, n, p, r, s,* and *t.*

For young children who are learning their letters, working out the alphabetic principle, and beginning to read and write independently, we offer this collection of poems to help them break the code.

Tessa's Toys

Tessa likes to line up her toys
And sing her own *ABC* song.
Sometimes she gets her friends to help.
Would you like to sing along?

A is for apple.
B is for boat.
C is for cat with a captain's coat.

D is for dog.
E is for elf.
F is for fan folded up on the shelf.

G is for goat.
H is for horn.
I is for inchworm measuring corn.

J is for juggler.
K is for kite.
L is for my lamp with its little light.

M is for moon shell.
N is for nest.
O is for octopus on a treasure chest.

P is for panda.
Q is for quail.
R is for robin that rests on a rail.

S is for sailboat.
T is for train.
U is for umbrella catching the rain.

continued

V is for valentine.
W is for wagon.
X is for xylophone and Xerxes the Dragon.

Y is for yo-yo, yellow yarn, and yak.
Z is for zebra with stripes on her back.
Now I know my *ABC*s.
Learning to read should be a breeze.

Tessa's Toys is meant to be sung to the tune of the *ABC* song. Learning this song is a first step to identifying letters for many young children. Just as they learn to count by rote before they can count items, they may learn to sing their *ABC*s before they can match names with letters.

The song helps children associate the letters whose names they are learning with words that begin with those letters—a first step in understanding the alphabetic principle that the letters we write stand for sounds that we say.

After learning about Tessa and her toys, children might like to try her game with their own toys. They may also enjoy making their own "toy catalogs" by cutting pictures from catalogs and advertisements or drawing pictures of their own and pasting them on the appropriate pages of a blank alphabet book. (If 26 letters are overwhelming, you might have them choose a few favorite letters or use some letters from their names.)

Children might also like to spend some time using letters as toys. They can match plastic letters with the letters on an alphabet strip, print with letter stamps, do alphabet puzzles, and build with alphabet blocks. One child we know liked to stick plastic letters into the "birthday cakes" he made from play dough. He learned the letter names as he played with them, just as he learned the names of the trucks, rubber animals, and other small objects that adorned his creations. One day, his caregiver noticed that he had chosen the letters *C*, *A*, and *T*. "You wrote cat!" she informed him, "*C-A-T*." His interest was piqued, so she gave him some stencils onto which he could place plastic letters to spell common words. This very young child was soon reading— and spelling—a handful of words. More important, he had learned through his play that he could put letters together to make words.

A E I O U

a, e, i, o, u
I can name them
So can you.
You can name them
So can I
It's not hard
If we just try.

This poem introduces children to the vowel sounds and gives them the opportunity to practice naming A, E, I, O, and U. The poem also includes at least one word with the long sound of each vowel (*name, we, I, so, you*) and at least one word with the short sound of each vowel (*can, them, it's, not, just*).

You might begin by teaching children to recite the poem with you as you point to the letters and words. Then see if they can find particular letters. Finally, talk with them about the vowel sounds. In the line "I can name them," can the children find a word where A "says its name?" Which letter in *can* makes the /a/ sound? In the next line, can they find the word *can*? Can they read the word *so*?

Letter Shapes

 has a big belly.

 is a cute curl.

's a duck;

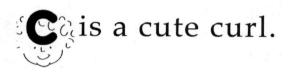's a flag.

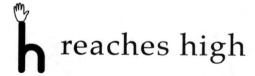's a gorgeous girl.

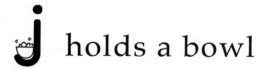 reaches high

To wave hello.

j holds a bowl

Of jiggly Jello.

continued

 is a kite

That flies up high.

is a line

Leading up to the sky.

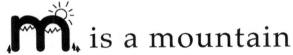 is a mountain

That has two humps.

 is a nice rounded hill

With no bumps.

continued

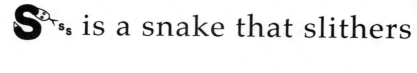

 puffs out his cheeks at cutie

 likes to rock and roll.

 is a snake that slithers

and shakes.

is a telephone pole.

 is a vase for violets.

 is a wide double vee.

 is for exxxxtra kisses.

 is the buzzzzzzzz of a bee.

continued

Learning the names and shapes of letters is a key step in figuring out the alphabetic principle that written words are made up of letters that correspond to spoken sounds. Because many of the letters have names that sound like their associated sound, children who can name letters can often read simple words or write with invented spelling (e.g., *cr* for *car* or *mt* for *empty*).

Tracing and eventually writing letters help children to get to know their names and to practice using them to create words that they—and eventually others—can read. As children write letters they like and labels and messages that are important to them, they are also practicing reading. In fact, having a well-stocked and effectively used "writing center" in a preschool classroom has been shown to make a difference in how easily the children learn to read in kindergarten and first grade.

Like reading, writing emerges over time. Young toddlers make marks on paper; older toddlers may draw lines or squiggles and say that they are writing. Gradually, preschoolers draw letterlike forms and eventually create "words" with some real letters. As children enter elementary school, their invented spelling and often inverted letters gradually become conventional writing. At the same time, children write with plastic letters, stamp pads, stickers, and computers. They begin by arranging or typing letters in random fashion and reading back what they think they wrote. Gradually, they learn how to put letters together into words that others can read.

Many preschoolers are particularly interested in learning to write their names so that they can sign their drawings and label their possessions. They may want to copy or trace letters and to practice writing on a slate or in the sand as well as on paper. We wrote this poem to help children who are developing an interest in writing "the grown-up way" remember the shapes of lowercase letters. As you help children who like the poem to form their letters, you can remind them to "make a big belly," "make two humps," or "make a vase for violets."

A is for Apple

A is for apple and acorns and art.
A is for acting when you take a part.

B is for butterfly, buttons, and boats.
B is for barely that you might eat with oats.

C is for cabbage and cornflakes and cow.
C is for clapping and taking a bow.

D is for dumpster and doughnuts and deer.
D is for dragons who should disappear.

E is for earring and eating and elf.
E is for everything I do by myself.

F is for fathers and feathers and fools.
F is for fish who go swimming in schools.

G is for gophers digging holes in the ground.
G is for giggling and goofing around.

H is for Halloween and hand-cream and hogs.
H is for heavy like a handful of logs.

I is for ice cream and iron and ice.
I is for itching that doesn't feel nice.

J is for jelly and juices and Jell-O.
J is for jester, a jocular fellow.

K is for kittens and kites that fly high.
K is for keeping the kites that you buy.

L is for lemon drops, licorice, and licks.
L is for lollipops and lollipop sticks.

M is for mousetraps and magic and mitts.
M is for morsels, or miniature bits.

N is for nothing, nobody, and none.
N is for not getting anything done.

O is for orange juice, orange trees, and ore.
O is for octopus, whose eight legs are sore.

P is for popcorn and peppers and pot.
P is for porridge that might be too hot.

Q is for quarrels and questions and quilt.
Q is for quarters that carpenters built.

R is for roses and relish and red.
R is for reading when you are in bed.

S is for sardines and starfish and sand.
S is for silk that feels soft in your hand.

T is for turkey to eat on Thanksgiving.
T is for the townhouse in which you are living.

U is for undies and ushers and us.
U is for upchuck when you're on a bus.

V is for violet and vivd and voom.
V is for vacuuming a very clean room.

W is for watching and waiting and word.
W is for whistling a song that you heard.

X is for x-rays that show you your bones.
X is in exit and xylophones.

Y is for yardsticks and yellow and yap.
Y is for yawning when it's time for your nap.

continued

Z is for zebras and zigzag and zone.
Z is for zooming to answer the phone.

These poems give children more practice with beginning sounds. Some children will enjoy brainstorming additional words that begin with each letter. A diverse collection of *ABC* books can help children find many different kinds of words—foods, flowers, toys, animals—even words in other languages or that have special significance in particular cultures.

One way to help children learn letters and their associated sounds is through simple games.

- "I spy something that starts with P. It's on the table and I can write on it. Can you guess what it is? It's a piece of P_____."

- "Look around the room. Do you see any Bs, like at the beginning of Bianca's name? What can we find that starts with a /b/ sound?"

- "Can you guess what nursery rhyme I'm saying? Back and Bill bent up the bill to betch a bail of bater. Can you say it using a T to start some of the words?"

- "Lets play the name game. We'll start with my name: Daddy, Daddy, bo-Baddy. Banana-fana fo-Faddy. Fee fi fo-Faddy. Daddy. Now let's do your name."

- "What would Devon's name be if it started with an M like Maria's?"

Children might also enjoy making collections of small objects whose names start with particular letters, planning meals with foods that start with a particular letter, or finding other children whose names start like theirs.

What Do You Know?

What can you say that begins with an *A*
Like anteaters and aardvarks that chase ants away?
I bet you know things that begin with a *B*
Like beach balls and big boats that float out to sea.

Can you call out some things that start with a *C*
Like candy and cauliflower and clocks with a key?
What did you discover that began with a *D*
Like donkeys and dinosaurs and dark dungarees?

What else do you know that begins with an *E*
Besides eagles and elephants eating excellent tea?
What's the first thing you think of that starts with an *F*
Like fresh fish filleted for a fine fancy chef?

What can you grow that begins with a *G*
Like grapes and gardenias and a great ginkgo tree?
Do you have pets at your house with an *H* in their names?
Does your horse eat his hay? Does your hamster play games?

Are you interested in things that begin with an *I*
Like iguanas and inchworms and nice ice cream pie?
Do you jump up for things that start with a *J*
Like jellies and junk food and jam on a tray?

Do you like to keep things that begin with a *K*
Like kittens and kangaroos kicking all day?
Do you love lots of things that begin with an *L*
Like licorice and lollipops that you lick so well?

Have you met any monkeys that begin with an *M*
Like marmosets and macaques that might mimic them?
Do you need some new things that begin with an *N*
Like notepads and note cards or a nib for your pen?

continued

What can you order that begins with an *O*
Like oatmeal and Oreos and orange juice to go?
Can you pick up some pies that begin with a *P*
Some peach pie for you and some pumpkin for me?

Do you have any questions about letter *Q*?
Did you know queens and quarters begin with *Q*, too?
Have you read about things that start with an *R*
Like a round rubber ring and a red racing car?

What can you see that begins with an *S*?
Sam slurping soda and making a mess!
Can you talk about things that begin with a *T*
Like a turtle, a tiger, and a tamarind tree?

Do you understand words that begin with a *U*
Like an ugly umbrella that's blocking the view
Of someplace I know that begins with a *V*—
A violet veranda overlooking the sea?

Want to know what begins with a *W*?
A walrus that would not want to trouble you!
I'm an expert on things that begin with an *X*
Like an extra-fast xebec with sails on its decks.

xebec

Do you know anything that begins with a *Y*?
In your yard you'll find something that catches your eye.
But watch out for sounds that start with a *Z*
Like the zing of a hornet or a mad, stinging bee.

When you've learned all these words and
you know how they start
Everyone will agree that you're really quite smart.

Writing a Letter

I would love to learn to write.
My dad showed me how the other night.
Somehow or other the pencil lead broke,
When I tried to make a downward stroke.

I asked my dad—nicely—to sharpen it,
But he said, "It's OK" and told me to sit.
I know I could write a much nicer letter,
If the pencil I write with would only write better.

I'm writing a letter to my big sister.
She went to college and I really miss her.
And I know how happy she will be,
When she receives a letter from me.

I know how to write, and I know how to spell,
But I don't do either very well.
My letter's all messy—I do not know why,
But my sister is happy whenever I try.

Writing letters or cards (or e-mail) gives writing a purpose. Here are some ways to help children send and receive "letters" even before they can read.

- Encourage children to draw pictures to share with friends and relatives and write or dictate notes on the back.

- Give children old greeting cards to play with and reuse.

- Put notes in children's cubbies or lunchboxes. Encourage them to put in pictures and "letters" to take home to their families.

- Set the font size on a word processor to 24 point (or larger). Let a child type with random letters and then "read" you the letter she wrote.

- Let children help you put stamps on letters and take them to the mailbox.

The Tale of Ed Word

I went out on a snowy day
And took my sled to the park to play.
Then Penelope said,
"There's an *ED* in that *SLED*."

I said, "My name is Ed,
But I'm not in a sled."
Then she picked up a stick
And said, "Watch this trick."

Penelope wrote *SLED*
With her stick in the snow.
She said, "*ED* is right
In there, you know."

She slid my sled
Across that *SLED*
Until I saw *LED*
And then saw *ED*.

We walked along
And found some b*oats*.
We saw that they were
Full of *oats*.

We climbed on board
The little t*rain*.
"Look!" she cried,
"It's full of *rain*."

"Thanks," I said.
"This game is neat!"
And then we found
The *tree* in st*reet*.

continued

It was time to go.
It was getting dark,
The *ark* in p*ark*.

I went back home.
It was time to eat.
What did I find?
A *bee* in my *bee*ts.

There was *ink* in my dr*ink*
And an *ape* in my gr*ape*s.
He drank *up* my c*up*
And *ate* from my pl*ate*s.

I ran to my room and found
A *pin* in my s*pin*ner
And some *sand* in a *sand*wich
Left over from dinner.

I discovered a *wag*
In my little toy *wag*on,
A *ring* in my st*ring,*
And a *rag* in my d*rag*on.

There was *jam* in my pa*jam*as
And a *pill* in my *pill*ow.
There was even an *arm*
In my *arm*adillo!

When Dad came in
To kiss me good night.
He said, "*Ed*, get in b*ed*
And I'll turn off the light."

continued

This poem was inspired by a young child who loved words, letters, and books and was just beginning to read on his own. One day, his aunt showed him that there was a *tree* in *street,* and he was totally fascinated.

Beginning readers can enjoy finding the hidden words in this poem as well as imagining things like *sand* in a *sandwich, jam* in *pajamas,* or an *ape* in *grapes.* They might also enjoy finding other words within words or starting with a simple word like *on* or *it* and seeing what words they can make by adding one or two letters at a time. Can they make words by adding letters at the end and at the beginning? Does adding some letters change the sound of the original word (as in *here* to *there* or *rang* to *range*)?

Silent E

Silent E has got the power, all right.
It can turn a *kit* into a kite.
It can turn a can into a cane
And even make a man a mane!
But in have and give and love and come—
E just sits there, feeling glum.

Silent letters are one of the quirks of English and of some other languages like French. In English, an **E** at the end of a four-letter word is almost always silent. In three-letter words with a consonant-vowel-consonant pattern, the vowel is usually short. Adding an **E** to the end of these words usually makes the first vowel long, as in *kit + e = kite*. Usually, but not always. The poem can help children remember the rule and some of its more common exceptions.

One way that children can have fun with the "silent *e*" rule is to make a word maker. Cut two parallel slots in an index card, one above the other, about an inch apart so that you can feed a strip of paper through them. On the strip, write the letters **F, H, M, P,** and **R**, spaced so that only one shows at a time when you pull the strip through the slot. On the card, write *ate*. Then make a flap that can cover up the **E**. Children can make different words by pulling the strip through and by lifting and lowering the flap. You can also create word strips with endings like *-an/-ane*, *-in/-ine*, *-it/-ite*, and *-op/-ope*. You can control the letters so that children can make only real words with correct spellings, or you can let them make some nonsense words and make up their own meanings. Either way, they will be getting good practice putting word parts together.

Katie Can!

Katie can do lots of things
Now that she is six.
She can shoot a basket
And do a lot of tricks.

She can feed her kitten.
She can fly a kite.
And when her pet gets sleepy,
She kisses him goodnight.

She comes into the kitchen
And packs a snack for school.
She can jump into the deep end
And kick across the pool.

She can say the alphabet
Or sing it as a song.
And when Ms. Kelly reads a book,
Katie reads along.

Kate keeps working every day
So soon she'll hear her father say,
"Everybody, shout 'Hooray!'
'Cause Katie can read!"

Learning to read is a bit like learning to ride a bike. Some children figure it out themselves through trial and error, but most need some pointers, some support, and lots of practice. All of the word play, vocabulary building, and pretend reading and writing, letter naming, listening to stories, and following the print as it is read aloud that children do helps prepare them to be fluent readers. Once they have mastered the sounds of letters and understand how these letters go together to make words, they still need lots of practice before they can read quickly enough for the words to make sense.

continued

For children learning letters, *Katie Can!* is full of **K** words. See how many the children can find. You might also point out that sometimes when you write the /k/ sound you write **K** (as in *Katie*), sometimes you write **C** (as in *can*), and sometimes, especially at or near the end of a word, you write **CK** (as in *tricks*). Do the children know any people whose names start with **K**? Or with a /k/ sound that is written with a different letter?

Many of the poems in this book, including this one, can be used to give beginning readers practice. Read the poem once through, then let the child try. If she gets stuck on a word, wait a bit to see if she can get it, then say the word for her. After you've gotten through the whole poem, you can go back and look at the words she had trouble with.

Be sure to celebrate each accomplishment along the way to independent reading. Once children can read on their own, however, don't stop reading with them. You can stretch their knowledge and skills by reading books that are a bit above their level and by discussing the story, the life lessons it teaches, and the techniques the author uses to engage and entertain her audience and to make certain points. You can get a child interested in a new book by reading its first page or chapter aloud or by taking turns reading pages.

Poems, especially, are meant to be read aloud and enjoyed together. We hope that the children in your care will continue to enjoy the spoken and written word as they build their literacy skills.

Appendix A

ABC Poems

Appendix B

Easy to Read Poems

Additional Copyright Information